Wicked
MOHAWK
VALLEY

Wicked
MOHAWK
VALLEY

DENNIS WEBSTER

Charleston · London

THE
History
PRESS

Published by The History Press
Charleston, SC 29403
www.historypress.net

Cover: Bird's-eye view of the city of Utica, Oneida County, New York, 1873.
Drawn by H. Brosius. *Library of Congress, Geography and Map Division.*

First published 2012

Manufactured in the United States

ISBN 978.1.60949.390.5

Library of Congress Cataloging-in-Publication Data

Webster, Dennis.
Wicked Mohawk Valley / Dennis Webster.
p. cm.
Includes bibliographical references.
ISBN 978-1-60949-390-5
1. Crime--New York (State)--Mohawk River Valley--History--Anecdotes.
2. Murder--New York (State)--Mohawk River Valley--History--Anecdotes.
3. Violence--New York (State)--Mohawk River Valley--History--Anecdotes. 4.
Mohawk River Valley (N.Y.)--History, Local--Anecdotes. 5. Mohawk River Valley
(N.Y.)--Biography--Anecdotes. I. Title.
HV6795.M6W43 2012
364.109747'6--dc23
2011045766

This book is dedicated to all the residents of the Mohawk Valley, who make the region a wonderful place to live, eat and breathe. For those reading this tome who do not reside in the Mohawk Valley, come and visit and you'll understand why this jewel of an area is among the most beautiful on our mother earth.

Contents

Preface   9
Acknowledgements   11
Introduction   13

The Notorious Swing from the Gallows   17
Cooking Your Husband Will Get You Hanged   22
The Young Demon Train Wreckers   30
No More Time to Tinker   37
Hello, Teacher, It's Nice to Kill You   42
A Lecture to the Ladies   55
Lumberjack Fugitive   59
Killed in the Bootleg War   62
The Dastardly Abortion Case   65
The Creeping Death   68
My, How the Sheriff's Garden Grows   73
The Chicken Roost Gang   76
His Numbers Didn't Add Up   78
What's On the Menu at Uncle Henry's Pancake House?   84
My Mommy the Axe Murderer   88
The Political Power Broker of Utica   92
Mr. Big   97
Dragged Behind a Car on Potato Hill Road   103

CONTENTS

Appendix A: The Mohawk Valley County Dossier   113
Appendix B: Map of the Mohawk Valley   117
Bibliography   119
About the Author   127

Preface

Iwant to assure the reader that I approached this book with the best intentions and without malice. I was born in the Mohawk Valley, completed my education here and am currently working, living and raising my family in the midst of this beautiful country. I have had offers in my life to relocate and turned them down. I have traveled all over the United States, and there is no better place to raise a family. The scenery is gorgeous, the food is an epicurean pleasure and my children are receiving a top-notch education. We have low crime and are a close drive to Canada, Boston and New York City. On top of all this, we have a diverse cultural base, with refugees from all over the world living in the valley. My great-grandparents came to this country and to the valley from across the sea. They came to improve their lives, and for choosing the Mohawk Valley, I am eternally grateful.

With all of this being said, I did write this book to show the other side of life in the Mohawk Valley—the dark side, the criminal side that we would like to wish away, but it's there, like a hangnail we can't pull. The Mohawk Valley is no different than any other community in the United States. About 99.9 percent of the people here are law-abiding and make our community the best. It's that other percentage that this book portrays, and it is by no means a smear against the entire region. I will live the rest of my life, die and will be buried in the rich soil of the Mohawk Valley, and for that I am fortunate.

Acknowledgements

I would like to thank my commissioning editor Whitney Tarella, as well as the staff at The History Press, for giving this book a home; the website www.fultonhistory.com, for its historical collection of newspaper archives; the Fulton County Historical Society; the Herkimer County Historical Society; the Oneida County Historical Society; the Utica Public Library; and individuals George Abel, Patricia Beck, Carol Hopson, Brian Howard, Bob Lalli, Bernadette Peck, Sue Perkins, Carl Saporito, Donna Terranova and Frank Tomaino. A loving thank-you goes to my parents, Charlene and Lee Webster, as well as my wife, Kelly, and our children—Ashley, Jakob and Stephanie—for their patience and understanding. An ever-grateful appreciation goes to my faithful first reader, Evelyn Webster. Without all of you, this book would not have been possible.

Introduction

The Mohawk Valley is a lengthy tract of land that slices between the Adirondack Mountains and the Catskill Mountains of Upstate New York. The region is a mixture of lush rural farmland, picturesque small towns and Americana villages and has a couple of small thriving cities in Rome and Utica. The Mohawk Valley started out as a popular travel route for those coming down from Canada and those from New York City going up the Hudson Valley toward the Great Lakes and the western territory. The original residents of the Mohawk Valley were the members of the Iroquois confederacy, also known as the Haudenosaunee or the "People of the Longhouse." These tribes were the Mohawk, Oneida, Onondaga, Cayuga and Seneca nations, who came together in alliance. They added the Tuscarora nation in 1722, coming to be known collectively as the Six Nations. This alliance was broken with the onset of the Revolutionary War when the Oneidas sided with the colonists under General Herkimer and fought and died against the British, as well as against some of their Iroquois brothers, at the Battle of Oriskany. Called the "Battle of Blood Creek," this action was considered a turning point in the war. The Mohawk Valley derives its name from the Mohawk tribe of the Haudenosaunee, who referred to themselves as the Kanien'keha'ka or "People of the Flint," a name based on their creation story of an arrow with a powerful flint.

The Mohawk Valley has always been a hub of people coming to this country to live the American dream of economic independence and freedom of thought. Dutch, French and English immigrants were the first

The Erie Canal was the travel hub of the burgeoning Mohawk Valley. The year was 1829, and the location was John Street in Utica, New York. *Oneida County Historical Society.*

wave, with the Irish, Polish, German, Welsh and Italian people all coming and settling in cities like Rome and Utica, helping swell the population and enhance the economic ascent of the area. With the completion of the Erie Canal in 1825, the Mohawk Valley now had a major water transportation system to move goods from New York City up the Hudson, through the heart of the territory and on to the Great Lakes, thus making the towns and cities along the canal in the Mohawk Valley strategically important in business and logistics.

The Mohawk Ford, by E.N. Clark. *Oneida County Historical Society.*

The Mohawk Valley blossomed in population, but along with the prosperity arose an underbelly of seedy humanity: crime (organized or not), prostitution, murder and other law-breaking offenses. The Mohawk Valley was also a prime location during prohibition for rumrunners coming down from Canada to New York City. In the shadows of the tall pines of the valley, criminal seeds were planted and sewn. To this day, the Mohawk Valley is a flavorful place, with Utica, New York, welcoming refugees fleeing oppression from all over the world and restaurants making homemade delights, while the crisp brooks overflow with brown trout. You can dig for diamonds in Herkimer, walk the hallowed ground of heroes at the Oriskany Battlefield and at Fort Stanwix in Rome and take your family to an abundance of parks, including the largest water park in New York State at Water Safari. It's within the beauty and grandeur of the Mohawk Valley that these historic, shocking crimes and insidious incidents took place.

The Notorious Swing from the Gallows

You're fixing me up like I'm going to a wedding.
— Virgil Jackson to law officers as he got dressed for his date with the noose

The following is a list of some of the executions delivered to nefarious killers and lawbreakers in the Mohawk Valley during the eighteenth and nineteenth centuries. Hangings would be replaced in the late nineteenth century by the more humane electric chair at Auburn Correctional Facility; however, the drama of the public hanging of criminals would never be equaled, as squads of citizens would turn out for the life-ending spectacle of watching the notorious swing from the gallows. These public displays were considered deterrents to crime, while humanitarians called them blood sports and abominations that equaled the crimes committed by the guilty.

SYLVIA WOOD, 1798

On April 29, 1798, Sylvia Wood (aka Sylvia Brown) came home to her house in Augusta drunk from a political party when her husband, Major Wood, attempted to subdue her. A fight ensued, with the major trying to restrain his wife, and she got hold of his pistol and fired it at her husband, gravely injuring the man. Major Wood died the next day, but not before he spoke to Peace Justice Thomas Cassely, telling him of his wife's shooting him in a drunken fit. A jury found her guilty of murder and sentenced her to hang, but Sylvia cheated the executioner by hanging herself in her jail cell.

GEORGE PETERS, 1801

Montauk Indian George Peters was a lost member of a coastal tribe of American Indians when he came to the Mohawk Valley and started his own tribe called the Brothertons. George ended up arrested and charged with murder in the death of his wife, Eunace Peters, in Rome, New York, on February 24, 1800. George killed his wife in an argument when he found her in a pub drunk with a man he suspected to be her lover. He repeatedly struck her on the head with a club until she was lifeless on the floor. George Peters was tried by jury at Fort Stanwix and found guilty. He was hanged in public on a tree branch in Whitesboro in August 1801.

JOHN TUHI, 1817

Brotherton Indian tribe member John Tuhi, seventeen, was found guilty of killing his older brother and fellow tribe member in a drunken fight. John struck his brother Joseph, nineteen, on July 25, 1817, with an axe in what was then the village of Utica. The two had been in the village of Clinton drinking at a pub. They returned to their home in a stupor, with Joseph asking his younger brother John to return the three cents that he owed. An argument on the debt escalated until John struck his brother with an axe. Joseph languished in pain for days before succumbing to his injuries. John Tuhi was tried in Rome, New York, and pleaded not guilty. John Tuhi was found guilty of murder and hanged in public in the area of the intersection of John and Rutger Streets in Utica, New York. The hanging was the first ever in Utica, with the event drawing a large crowd. Today his spirit is said to walk the grounds of the mansions along Rutger Street, seeking solace from the murder of his long-dead brother.

MARY RUNKLE, 1847

The life of Mary Runkle was filled with malfeasance and ended with her neck snapped at the end of the executioner's rope. Mary's life of crime had started with a charge of stealing seat cushions from a church in Fulton and continued with several charges for minor offenses until a few murder charges were put forth: drowning one of her children in a tub that had two inches of water in it; killing a peddler who came to her house; and poisoning her son, whom she claimed had the measles. But the last murder charge was the one that carried her to her maker: the strangling and beating death of her husband.

Mary's eleven-year-old daughter testified that her mother had made her hold her father's legs down while she clasped her hands over the man's throat until froth came from his mouth. Mary claimed that she had been pulled by the hair and beaten by her husband and that she had waited on him hand and foot, with him getting upset at her serving him spoiled milk (he drank brandy instead). Mary went on to say that she blew a candle out at 1:00 a.m. and lay down in bed next to her husband, who then proceeded to attack her. She claimed that she was only defending herself. A jury was not convinced, found her guilty of murder and sentenced her to capital punishment by hanging.

The execution took place in Whitesboro, New York, and had one thousand citizens in attendance despite a heavy downpour of rain. Right before the execution, it was reported that Mary needed assistance getting dressed and only mumbled in her cell that she had made peace with her maker. She was led to the gallows and sat in a chair under the noose while a prayer was recited. She closed her eyes and leaned her head on her jailer. When asked if she had anything to say to the witnesses or her jury, Mary remained silent. She was stood up from the chair and led to the hatch door. She had her hands bound, and the noose was placed around her neck and tightened. At 1:00 p.m., a bell was rung, and the supporting rope was cut, causing Mary Runkle to fall through. She hanged silent for twenty minutes before the jailers cut her down and placed her body in a coffin, which was carried off by family and friends. The reporters of the time were shocked at the execution of a woman, for it was rare that any female would be in any kind of trouble with the law, let alone be executed for murder.

Virgil Jackson, 1888

On January 28, 1888, Virgil Jackson shot and killed Norton Metcalf in Augusta Center after attending church services with Metcalf's wife. Virgil was walking Mrs. Metcalf home from church when Mr. Metcalf came out into the road in front of his house and accused Jackson of having an affair with his wife. Jackson took out a pistol and shot Norton Metcalf three times before the man slumped to the ground in a heap. One shot was through the heart, another through the shoulder and the last one through the chest. Law officers went to Jackson's home to arrest him and found Mrs. Metcalf's undergarments in his dresser drawers.

In the trial, it came out that Virgil Jackson had a lengthy criminal history and an affinity for being a lothario toward the ladies. Although he was married with children, Jackson had fathered multiple children with other women and even had a charge laid against him that he had forced a young pregnant woman to commit to an abortion. This revelation stunned the courtroom. Frederick Wasooth, who owned a store next door to the Metcalfs, witnessed the shooting through his window. He testified that he saw Mr. Metcalf and Virgil Jackson in the road, with Mrs. Metcalf standing behind Jackson. He saw Jackson level his pistol, witnessed a flash, heard a report and saw smoke, all of which was repeated twice. Metcalf took a few steps and fell to the ground. Wasooth then testified that Jackson carried Metcalf's body into the house.

George Metcalf, the son, testified that his parents hadn't slept in the same bed for some time. He openly wept on the stand. The jury found Jackson guilty of murder and sentenced him to hang until dead. By this time, capital executions in New York State were no longer done in public, so Jackson was hanged in the fenced-in Bleecker Street Jail yard in Utica. The hanging was scheduled for March 15, 1889. It was reported that on the day of the execution, Jackson asked if he could take a bath in his cell, which was granted. He had his jailers assist him in getting dressed in new clothes and said, "You're fixing me up like I'm going to a wedding." Before he was brought to the gallows outside, Jackson had no idea that a hearse wagon with a coffin was sitting in the barn waiting to take his body away. The undertaker was standing in the doorway with his hands clasped in front of his body. Jackson was taken up the stairs and sat in a chair underneath the noose and directly over the trapdoor. He was asked if he had anything to say, and he shook his head. Jackson was stood up, the chair was removed and straps were placed around his elbows and knees, with the hangman placing a black hood over his head. Although the witnesses were only a few dozen lawmen and politicians in the jail yard, citizens crowded in trees and roofs around the perimeter, attempting to witness the execution. They put the noose around Jackson's neck and snugly fit it before pulling the lever and sending him downward, which snapped his neck instantly. Virgil Jackson was the last execution in Oneida County.

Cooking Your Husband
Will Get You Hanged

Weep not, dear child, for me when I am gone
for life has so little pleasure at the best for me.
—Roxalana Druse in a jailhouse letter to her daughter, Mary,
on the evening before her execution

WARREN, NEW YORK, 1884

Roxalana Druse had married her husband, William Druse, when she was twenty-two years old, and the young lass had cause for trepidation—the odd man with the long beard was thirty-eight years old, a difference that she later admitted to her sister, Lucy, was probably too much of a divide. It was the culmination of twenty years of hard labor on the farm in Warren, as well as the physical abuse at the hands of her husband, that would lead to Roxalana's mental meltdown, ending in her murdering him. Some would say that it was self-defense. The death of William Druse on a cold December morning in 1884 led to one of the most sensational trials in the history of the Mohawk Valley, and her ultimate guilt would be proven by Dr. A. Walter Suiter of Herkimer, New York, who would use a new methodology that we now refer to as forensics.

What led a hardworking, respectable woman to kill a fellow human being? What led Roxalana to murder her husband, chop his head off, hack the rest of him to pan-sized pieces and cook him in the stove, burying his remnants in the soil of her farm? The answer is what we would refer to in this day and

Roxalana Druse. *Herkimer County Historical Society.*

age as spousal abuse or battered wife syndrome. Life was hard for Roxalana and her children—Mary, nineteen, and George, nine—at the time of their father's death. Their small farmhouse sat on ninety acres of land that was tough to till. The Central New York winters battered their tattered house, and Mary was married twenty years to a person neighbors described as an "oddball" of a man who tinkered, was lazy and poor and barely spoke to people when they visited. Mary later testified that her father had beaten her mother on many occasions.

The morning of the murder had Roxalana entertaining her nephew, Frank Gates, fourteen, who was there to assist with chores on the farm. Roxalana's sister, Lucy Gates, lived down the road from the Druse farm. George and Frank had gone outside to do chores, while Roxalana and Mary stayed in to prepare breakfast. It was at this point that the lads outside heard yelling. They looked in, and George described seeing his mother on the end of violent blows from his father. At this point, in her shame and embarrassment, Roxalana asked her son to go back outside and around the corner. Revolver shots rang out in the early morning cold, echoing throughout the area. George later testified that his mother came outside, retrieved an axe, chopped off his father's head and wrapped it in cloth. The rest of the body was chopped up and cooked on the parlor stove.

When law authorities came to the farm to question Roxalana, she claimed that her husband had left the family and had gone to New York City; however, Jeremiah Eckler, a neighbor, dug up the bones, kept them at his home and then turned them over to the authorities. Roxalana swore that they had dog bones, but it didn't deter the authorities, who had decided to put her on trial for the murder of her husband. The trial and aftermath expanded the drama to something never before seen in the history of the Mohawk Valley and led to the repeal of public criminal hangings in New York State. Three years after the hanging of Roxalana, New York State began using its new, more humane device for the execution of criminals: the electric chair. The trial featured Dr. A. Walter Suiter of Herkimer, New York, employing criminal investigative techniques never before seen. Dr. Suiter enthralled the courtroom with his description of sifting out the bone fragments that he identified as human, as well as his hands-on experimentation with the home cremation of William's body, going into great detail on the amount of wood fuel it would take to completely cook and dissolve certain pounds of human flesh. He had removed the stove from the Druse farm in his flesh-cooking experiments. His workings were documented in medical papers that were placed in Albany.

DeWight Luce was assigned to be Roxalana's defense lawyer and had to follow the compelling testimony of Dr. Suiter to an overflowing courtroom in September 1885 in Herkimer, New

William Druse. *Herkimer County Historical Society.*

York. In a move that was rare in its day, Luce used the defense of spousal abuse as reasoning for the dastardly deed. He brought forth Mary Druse to testify that her mother was beaten and had killed William out of fear for her own life. Women were not able to vote until 1920 and in many places of the United States were on the same level as common property like a fence post or a mule. It would be a dramatic move that would keep the entire courtroom spellbound. According to Luce, the homicide was justified. Mary testified that her father beat her mother continuously and in front of her and her little brother, George. One time, William gave Roxalana lashings with a horsewhip. Mary explained with great emotion how her mother was beaten on the morning of the death of her father and that her mother had wild eyes. William had come out to breakfast angry and exploded at Roxalana, punching her in the face for making bad tea. According to Mary, he then got a knife and threatened to kill her mother, so Roxalana pulled out a revolver and put a round into William. The finishing death blow came via the axe that removed the abusive man's head from his shoulders.

The defense rested with DeWight Luce's passionate plea for mercy toward Roxalana. Judge Pardon Williams instructed the jury to determine if the death of William Druse was to be excused due to the testimony and stated that William's cruel behavior toward his wife didn't necessitate murder. The judge stated that the jury needed to determine if Mrs. Druse had been in peril enough that she had no choice but to shoot her husband. The jury took no more than five hours to find Roxalana guilty of murder in the first degree, and Judge Williams sentenced her to hang by the neck until dead. This sentence was given in November 1885, yet it took years for the final execution to take place.

Appeals were filed by attorney Luce, and for many months after the original sentencing, Roxalana sat in the Herkimer County Jail, although the jailers allowed her to have a bed, a dresser, a rocking chair and other personal accoutrements. It was the final appeal before Judge George Hardin that would seal her mortal fate, as the judge deemed that the trial had been fair. All Luce could do now was appeal to the governor of New York for clemency or lobby the legislature to change the laws to no longer allow capital punishment. Roxalana had friends in the clergy and in women's advocacy groups who wrote letters on her behalf to the governor asking for clemency. Thousands of letters poured in, and the Woman Suffrage Organization of New York State stated that Roxalana was a member of the society and that she should not be executed based on the fact that women were oppressed and were denied rights. New York governor David B. Hill sent a team to examine Mrs. Druse's sanity to placate those who wanted her committed to an insane asylum, yet she was deemed fit to be executed. The only delay was the governor giving the legislature time to pass a law making the execution of women in New York State illegal. This law failed, so Roxalana was due to

Roxalana's children, George and Mary Druse. *Herkimer County Historical Society.*

be hanged on February 28, 1887. The governor with presidential aspirations declared that he'd rather not be president of the United States than grant clemency to Roxalana Druse.

Mary Druse, for her assistance in the death of her father, was charged with second-degree murder, for which she pleaded guilty. Roxalana insisted until her execution that Mary had nothing to do with the death of William. Judge Williams sentenced Mary to prison for the rest of her natural life. She was sent to the Onondaga County Penitentiary and spent one decade there. She was briefly transferred to Auburn State Prison until she was pardoned by New York governor Levi Morton. Even though she was only twenty-eight years old upon her release, it was said that Mary never recovered from her despair at the execution of her beloved mother.

Roxalana's last night alive on this earth was one of heartbreak and terror. It was Sunday, February 27, 1887, and she sat in angst until the arrival of Reverend George W. Powell, along with the choir from his Universalist church. Reverend Powell was alone with Roxalana in her jail cell, and the kindness shown to Roxalana by Sheriff Cook continued with his allowance of the service. Sheriff Cook and his wife had supplied Roxalana with the rocking chair that she sat in while awaiting her fate. The reverend conducted the service, with the choir in the other room breaking out into "We Shall Move on that Beautiful Shore," a song chosen by Roxalana. She sang along in her beautiful voice that was hours away from being silenced. At 10:30 p.m., she sat alone and sipped a bowl of oyster stew with relish. At 11:00 p.m., she was trying to stay calm when she became excited and wept. She drank some brandy and fell asleep from 11:30 p.m. to 1:00 a.m. and was reported by Sheriff Cook to be talking in her sleep, uttering phrases like "The woman must bang the gates and go free," "They think they have Bill's bones, but they've dog bones" and "He thinks he is better than I am, but he will find out."

Roxalana wept as she sat up for hours, writing goodbye letters to George and Mary, as well as letters of appreciation to several people, including Deputy Manion and Sheriff Cook. Her goodbye letter to Mary was published in the *Syracuse Daily Courier*:

Mary,

I shall have this letter buried with me if I die but I hope that a kind reader from above will whisper softly in the governor's ear and let me live. Dearest Child, if no such message comes do not grieve for me, be brave, for I have

The *National Police Gazette of New York* shows a collage of drawings depicting the last day on earth for Roxalana Druse. *Old Fulton New York Post Cards, fultonhistory.com.*

suffered everything but death for what others ought to, and if I die I shall be at rest. Weep not, dear child, for me when I am gone for life has so little pleasure at the best for me. It is nearly 3 o'clock of night. I have willed my body to Mr. Powell and he will take care of it. He will write you in a day or two. He brought the choir here this evening to sing for me. They sang several nice pieces and I enjoyed it very much. I am more than thankful and to the Reverend and Mrs. Powell for kindly coming. In a time of need Mrs. Powell is a kind and very pleasant lady. Goodbye, my dearest, dear girl, and may some power spring up in your life's pathway to obscure the darkness that clouds it. Farewell is my last dying words is all I can say, to my dear daughter I love so well.

Mrs. Roxalana Druse

Roxalana stayed awake until 6:30 a.m. and then woke up at 7:00 a.m. and got dressed in her black silk dress, the same one that she had worn to her trial. Roxalana had P.R. Witherstine, editor of the *Herkimer Democrat* and notary public, draw up an affidavit in which she swore that Mary had nothing to do with her father's death. She then removed a necklace that was described in the paper at the time as "old fashioned" and handed it to her jailer, Mr. Terry, saying, "Here is the last token I can send Mary. Give it to her and tell her to wear it always." Reverend Powell arrived at 9:30 a.m. to stay with her until the end. At 11:00 a.m., Chaplain Durston of the Onondaga Penitentiary came and held services in Roxalana's cell with Reverend Powell. The chaplain also delivered a bouquet of flowers that Mary had sent to her mother. This caused her to weep in sorrow.

What caused Roxalana to break down even more was the sound of drums being thumped outside to a military beat. The hanging would be held in the yard of the Herkimer County Jail, which was fenced in to keep the massive number of onlookers from witnessing the event. The Mohawk Rifles, sixty-four men in number, patrolled the fence with military precision while drumming along in their thick overcoats and knapsacks, while the National Guard and several court deputies kept the massive crowd at bay. Citizens crammed on nearby rooftops and in the windows of the courthouse during the chilly February morning in hopes of watching the hanging. Massive public hangings had been declared unacceptable by New York State, so only a dozen citizens were chosen to witness the hanging, although the courtyard was full of lawmen and reporters. People filled the village of Herkimer as if it were a national holiday. Sheriff Cook had kept a tight rein on who exactly was allowed in the courtyard, with the Herkimer County judge not being allowed inside until Sheriff Cook approved.

The gallows that were to break the neck of Roxalana Druse were constructed out of hardwood and didn't have a trapdoor like most such devices, but rather a weight would come to earth upon release and would take Mrs. Druse from standing at ground level into the air above the crowd, so even the courtyard witnesses farthest away would be able to see her wriggle to the last breath. The device had been previously used for criminal hangings, and Sheriff Cook had it repainted in black-and-white striping.

Roxalana came out of the Herkimer County Jail carrying the flowers sent by her loving Mary. At the sight of the gallows, she became weak in the knees and had to be held up. Once at the platform, she knelt down with Reverend Powell and prayed. She then had the flowers taken away, a hood placed over her head and straps wrapped around her body to keep her from trying to free herself or from flailing about too much under the noose. It was 11:48 a.m. when the executioner pulled the pin, and she was pulled up toward heaven. It took several minutes before she was declared dead by strangulation. As promised, Reverend Powell took possession of her body and placed the flowers from Mary on the casket as it was led away. Roxalana Druse would be one of the last people hanged in New York State and the last woman in Herkimer County. Her body was buried in an unmarked grave at Oak Hill Cemetery on a slope, west of the village of Herkimer. Roxalana's ghost has been rumored to walk the hallways, staircases and courtroom at the historic Herkimer County Courthouse.

The Young Demon Train Wreckers

Mercy pleaded with Justice and the blind goddess balanced her scales.
—anonymous reporter of the Saturday Globe, *Utica, New York*

ROME, NEW YORK, NOVEMBER 1895

John Watson Hildreth had just turned seventeen years old and was living in Rome, New York, biding his time reading his beloved dime store novels that sensationalized everything from the Wild West to bank robberies. One that caught his fancy was the story of the daring desperado Oliver Curtis Perry, who had robbed a train in Central New York and stolen a locomotive to use as his getaway. It was this serialization that led to one of the most severe criminal cases in nineteenth-century Oneida County. John Watson Hildreth had come from a prominent and religious New York City family, with his father having been a lawyer. John had told his father that he was attending agricultural school in the Mohawk Valley, and his father, pleased with John's direction, sent him tuition money to make his path in this world, yet John spent all of his spare money on dime store novels.

It was after reading about Oliver Curtis Perry that Hildreth plotted the wrecking and robbery of a train—a feat that would make him and his best pals filthy rich. Hildreth had shared wild stories with Herbert Plato, Theodore Hibbard, Fred Bristol and Joseph Wilkes. All of the boys were idealistic teenagers, their entire lives ahead of them, or so it seemed.

The boys who wrecked the train. *Top, left to right*: John Watson Hildreth and Herbert Plato. *Bottom, left to right*: Theodore Hibbard and Fred Bristol. *Oneida County Historical Society.*

The lads decided to live the life of the dime store novels they adored, to crash a train and rob the passengers at gunpoint. They would take the booty from the passengers and kill whoever survived the wreck. They planned on going out west with their newfound riches and living the easy life. When it came time to buy the guns and move the plot forward, Joseph Wilkes backed out, his cowardly yet instinctual smarts saving him and his family lifelong grief. The four remaining lads went together and purchased their revolvers to use in the holdup.

The lads gathered together in the early morning of November 10, 1895, and walked the tracks west of Rome, New York, getting farther into the desolate western swampland, where only the wildlife of the woods and wetlands were witness to their deeds. They came upon a toolshed and broke in to find a pry bar and hammer, with Plato stating that he'd use the hammer to dispense any survivors if his revolver were·to misfire. The young men spent the next hour prying and removing a handful of rails. The sun was coming up, and the train was coming from Syracuse toward Rome. The boys had timed it perfectly. They sprinted down the fifteen-foot embankment and hid behind a thicket of trees, revolvers at the ready.

Nathan N. Hager had been a locomotive engineer for more than forty years and loved nothing better than pulling the chain on the train whistle every time he'd pass his parents' home, which was built close to the tracks where he made his life's work. It was while driving the machine he loved that this soft-spoken engineer would meet his demise. The train was going fifty miles per hour, was filled with U.S. mail and had several sleeping cars at the back end, with dozens of dozing passengers. He came around the bend and saw what no engineer ever wants to see: rails missing. It was later reported by Chris Wagner, the fireman who was riding by Hager's side, that the brave engineer, upon seeing the missing tracks, declared, "My God," as he desperately tried to halt the train. However, the millions of pounds of steel and moving wheels couldn't have had its momentum halted even by the Almighty himself. The train hit the missing rail spot and lurched down the steep embankment as it dove deep into the muck and mud of the swamp, sliding nose down for three hundred feet, followed by the cars plowing into and flipping over one another. Nathan N. Hager was killed instantly, yet Wagner miraculously lived to tell the story. Only one other person was killed: Robert Bond, a worker who was not assigned to work on this run but was taking a ride to another location. He was not even supposed to be on this train.

THE BOYS ACCUSED OF WRECKING THE NEW YORK CENTRAL TRAIN.

HERBERT PLATO.   JOSEPH WILKES   J. WATSON HILDRETH   FRED BRISTOL   THEODORE HIBBARD

A rogue's gallery of the Young Demon Train Wreckers.

Upon seeing the wreck, the cowardly would-be robbers hiding behind the trees fled the scene, lacking the fortitude to complete their dastardly deed. They didn't stay around to see a multitude of passengers moaning with injuries, crying out in pain or down on their knees in the swamp, praying. The lads tossed their revolvers into a patch of swamp water as they made their way back to population. Firefighters, police officers and citizen volunteers responded to the massive wreckage, with everyone mourning the deaths of the two men yet amazed that there were not more who had passed into the hands of God. Detective John Latham of the Central New York Railroad was walking the wreckage later that day when a volunteer approached and handed him a hat that had been found nearby in a patch of woods. He looked inside the hat, and written clearly was the name "Hildreth." It was the very leader himself who would discover his missing hat and return later that night to retrieve it. Detective Latham and Rome police officer Kingsley were walking the path near the wreck the night the young man walked up to them carrying a lit lantern on a stick that was flung over his shoulder. Upon questioning the young man, the officers placed Hildreth under arrest.

Once back at the police station, Hildreth confessed and implicated the other young men, who were then rounded up and placed under arrest. Hildreth, the leader, was seventeen years old; Bristol and Hibbard were eighteen years old; and Plato was nineteen. Authorities were shocked at the youthful appearance of the perpetrators and also that none of them had ever committed a single crime in their young lives. It was only a few months in jail before Fred Bristol, who had been in poor health, died of consumption. The trial would be the costliest ($8,000)

JOHN WATSON HILDRETH.
(Sentenced for Life.)

HERBERT PLATO.
(Sentenced to Forty Years' Imprisonment.)

Hard labor in prison awaited the teenagers.

and most sensationalized in the history of the Mohawk Valley, with a packed courtroom filled with relatives of victims and those charged, as well as lawmen and reporters from dozens of newspapers from around New York State. Presiding over the case was Justice Peter B. McLennan, the prosecutor was Oneida County district attorney George S. Klock and the defense attorney was someone considered at the time to be one of the brightest defense attorneys in the territory: Joseph Sayles of Rome, New York. The grand jury convened and indicted the young men on thirty-one counts, including murder in the first degree, for which a guilty verdict could result in the lads being placed to cook in the electric chair.

Prominent at the trial were the reporters from the *Globe* of Utica, which gave front-page coverage to the sensational trial. These anonymous reporters stated in writing the following about the young men: "They were bright looking and not the looks of criminals." Yet they gave to the young men the moniker "Young Demon Train Wreckers" and claimed that the lads had "carried away the championship for deviltry." Hildreth's love of dime store novels came out in the trial, especially his infatuation with the serialized story of the train robber Oliver Curtis Perry, whom the ringleader used as inspiration for his crime. The prosecution had a quick case in bringing forth the confessions of the young men, as well as a witness in Cella Perrin, toward whom Hildreth had a romantic inclination. She lived in the same boardinghouse as Hildreth, who confessed to her his involvement in the train wreck. Her testimony ended a strong case, leaving the defense with not much to do but call in witnesses who claimed to have been with the lads when the wreck occurred. The defense also brought into court a rotten railroad tie that had come from a pile near the wreck. The defense tried to claim that the rails had gone askew from the wooden ties rotting out from underneath and not due to an insidious plot by well-behaved young men. It did not take long for the jury of thirteen men to come back with a guilty verdict for Hildreth. This caused Plato and Hibbard to plead guilty for manslaughter in the first degree.

Hildreth's sentence came first, while Plato and Hibbard sat in an adjacent room. Hildreth was given a life of hard labor at Auburn State Prison, thus saving him from the electric chair. Family members sobbed as the slight young man was led away in shackles, and then the other conspirators came into the courtroom. Plato and Hibbard both appealed for clemency and mercy from the court. Judge McLennon said to the lads, "The court cannot impose less than the maximum sentence of the law. This crime of which you both pled guilty is most terrible. It strikes at the root in our civilization." He then went on to say, "Be good boys in prison not bad boys." They were then both sentenced to forty years' hard labor at Auburn State Prison. Family members of the guilty and victims alike wept.

The three lads were taken by Sheriff Weaver to Auburn State Prison by train. The train halted right at the front gate of the prison in Auburn, New York, to throes of people gawking at the guilty young men, with many gasping at the youthful appearances and boyish sizes of the Demon Train Wreckers. Many stated that they looked like children. The three lads were shackled together and had to march through the gathered crowd and past the large wrought-iron gate of the prison. It was reported that Hildreth appeared frightened, Hibbard looked curiously around and Plato was smiling and smirking. Reporters were allowed to come into the prison to witness the processing of the three boys. The lads were stripped of their civilian garb and given striped prison uniforms. After donning the uniforms, the boys were weighed and measured as if they were livestock. Hildreth weighed 116 pounds and was five feet tall; Hibbard weighed 140 pounds and was five feet, five inches tall; and Plato weighed 136 pounds and was five feet, three inches tall. They were then given a printout of the prison rules, and since all three had been common school educated, they were able to read them on their own. When Warden Stout was asked about the boys, he stated that he was shocked at how young they looked and that he hadn't yet decided what work they would be performing, so for the meantime he had sent them to their prison cells.

No More Time to Tinker

No, no, NO!!!
—the last earthly words of Judge William E. McLachlan
as he was stabbed repeatedly by his killer

Judge William E. McLachlan loved to tinker more than he loved mediating justice from his bench. He had been the justice of the peace in Amsterdam for eight years, but it was the turn of the twentieth century and he'd had enough of the foolish cases before him, so he gave it all up to tinker with clocks and live the simple life of a hermit. His home on Cranes Hollow Road, high on a knoll surrounded by sixty-five acres of pristine farmland just outside the town of Cranesville, was filled with the timekeeping devices, so many in number that the former judge had one room that served as his kitchen, workshop, dining room and sleeping apartment. He had clocks stacked to the ceiling, as well as tools and parts strewn about that occupied every nook and cranny of his old farmhouse. In one large room, he had many different types of clocks covering every inch of the walls, with many distinctive chimes ringing out. It was among his clocks, on Tuesday, July 23, 1907, that this hermit tinker, after thirty years of seclusion, would meet his grisly demise.

Judge McLachlan, although a recluse for many decades, did enjoy repairing clocks for an assortment of customers, even modern early twentieth-century models. It was in this service capacity that his body was discovered. On a fateful hot Tuesday in July, Mrs. Fort and Mrs. Gardinied had gone together to pick up clocks that they had left with the judge to be repaired. Upon arrival to the farmhouse on the hill, they knocked and called out for the tinker, with no response, so the ladies sallied forth down the country road until they came upon a man fishing for brown trout in a creek. It was George Brewster, the seventy-nine-year-old neighbor who had known Judge McLachlan for many years yet was not close to him. The judge had preferred to keep to himself. George put aside fishing for his lunch to assist the ladies in their quest for their clocks.

George and the ladies walked to the pond behind the judge's house, expecting to see him there fishing, yet there was nobody about. They then went into the house and ventured farther inside, calling out, "Gene!" which was what the neighbors called the hermit. There was no response. Finally they found the judge, facedown on the floor in a pool of blood. He was dead. There was blood smeared all over the doorframe to the back room, where McLachlan had a stash of weapons, including loaded muskets, double breechloaders and rifles. One weapon had blood on it, as if the judge had fought valiantly to get to his guns to defend himself. The three who found him walked outside and went for the sheriff.

Deputy Sheriff William J. Munsell arrived along with Coroner Tim Merman and discovered that Judge William Eugene McLachlan had died of multiple stab wounds and blunt-force trauma to the head. The coroner listed the cause of death as murder. The sheriff didn't think that the cause of death was from a robbery gone awry, for the judge had a purse on his body that had money in it, as well as his gold watch, although with the sheer amount of clutter and hoarded items, it would be difficult to tell what was missing. It was thought that it must have been a struggle with somebody the judge had known, for there was no forced entry. The coroner took the body of the judge with him and delivered it to Undertaker Lutton's morgue.

By the evening, Detective Bergen and District Attorney Maxwell had joined Sheriff Munsell to guard the house overnight. It was one o'clock in the morning and the lawmen were sitting on the front porch of the judge's residence, listening to the peaceful chirping of the crickets, when they heard gunfire. Four distinct shots rang out in the night. Soon, Deputy Sheriff McGlauchlin from the Fonda Sheriff's Office came up the driveway on his horse and buggy. He explained that he had been a quarter mile down the road driving along under the moonlight when he came upon two men walking down Cranes Hollow Road. Both sides of the road had thick forest, and when the men saw the sheriff, they bolted into the brush. He jumped from his buggy and gave chase, yelling out, "Halt!" When the men refused to comply, he cracked off four shots at them. He wasn't sure if his bullets hit their marks, but he lost the men. It was at this point that the entire group went looking for these men, but they were unable to find them.

In the morning, the lawmen looked over the judge's home and discovered a pile of valuable goods that seemed out of place. There were two small hand organs, a nickel-in-the-slot Regina music box, a stack of phonographic records and a pile of new buckskin gloves. The judge had been a miser yet was deemed to have goods of high value, as well as more than $85,000 in cash. The judge's brother had told the lawmen that although his brother was a hermit, he had lamented about never having met a woman or falling in love. He had denied himself all pleasures in his life, yet the judge wasn't able to take his beloved clocks with him to the afterlife.

It did not take long for the lawmen to arrest two young men and charge them with the murder. John Cincotta and Joseph Gervasio were identified by Nicholas Young as having been on Cranes Hollow Road at the time of the murder. This was verified by the testimony of a young girl, Lillie Dennis, who had seen both men at the same date and time. In what was a simple trial, both men were convicted, with Cincotta being found guilty of murder in the second degree and receiving twenty years and Gervasio being found guilty of manslaughter and receiving fifteen years. During this trial and afterward, the drama reached new heights.

Both men swore that there was a mastermind, yet they were sent to Dannemora State Prison. Little did they know that the authorities believed their story. The two convicted killers had stated that Frank Denatto of Amsterdam had paid them $750 to go to Judge McLachlan's farmhouse and retrieve papers that Denatto had signed showing that he had borrowed $2,000 from the judge. Cincotta and Gervasio had sworn that they were playing cards with Denatto in the back room of the saloon he ran in Amsterdam when he asked them to do him a favor for $500. He asked them to kill the judge and not to tie him up. The men negotiated the pay to $750, and Denatto explained where the farmhouse was and where the papers would be. The men admitted that they had killed the man, with Cincotta stabbing the judge multiple times while Gervasio stood back with a pistol in his hand and watched. The old man was screaming, "No, no, NO!!!" as the knife was plunged again and again into his torso.

With this testimony, Judge Charles Tobin of Fonda issued the warrant for the arrest of Frank Denatto, charging him with murder in the first degree. When Deputy Sheriff McGlauchlin, Detective Neef, Chief of Police Bartlett and Detective Bergen of Amsterdam arrived to arrest Denatto, they were treated to tense moments and high drama. Denatto's daughter stood her ground in front of the home, while her father was inside. She was hysterical and was ripping her hair out, screaming that they'd never take her father alive. It was at this time that numerous friends and family arrived and stood between the lawmen and the Denatto homestead. When the tension hit its peak, Frank Denatto calmly came out of the house and asked his daughter to settle down. He asked to see the warrant and surrendered himself to the authorities. He claimed that he was innocent of the charges.

The trial of Frank Denatto began as soon as John Cincotta and Joseph Gervasio arrived via train from their prison sentences. They were the star witnesses in the trial and were housed on the second floor of the Fonda County Jail. On June 1909, the two men made a jail break that put the entire state of New York on high alert. The men had dug a hole through the second-floor wall that was eighteen inches thick, and when the deputies found their empty cell, they also discovered a rope tied to the bed running out of the hole. It was on the side of the wall facing the Mohawk River, so it was not seen from the road. At the base of the jail, next to the rope, was their prison garb in a pile. It was obvious that somebody had helped the men escape. The townsfolk hunkered down in their homes from the news that the two convicted murderers were on the loose. Many were whispering that the Black Hand Society had assisted in the escape, yet there was no proof that such a society existed let alone had assisted in their escape. The next day, Joseph Gervasio was found hiding under an apple tree on the Akin property of William Marshall Sr., who just happened to live next door to Judge Lepper. Marshall escorted the escapee into Lepper's home, and it was discovered that the man had rope burns on his palms from the escape. Cincotta was picked up walking the streets of Amsterdam shortly thereafter.

Even with the testimony of both Cincotta and Gervasio, the jury came back and found Frank Denatto not guilty, a turn of events that spread shock throughout New York State, although Denatto's daughter couldn't hide her glee and was scolded by Judge Spencer for her outlandish display. Spencer also admonished the jury members for their incompetence and declared them of unfit character, but the decision had been rendered. Gervasio and Cincotta were escorted by lawmen back to Dannemora State Prison via train. They told reporters on the train that they had indeed committed the crime but that a guilty man had gone free. Cincotta lamented, "That was a nice jury. I wish when I was tried on the same charge as Frank Denatto I had the same kind of fool jury."

Hello, Teacher, It's Nice to Kill You

Even God almighty don't know what a jury will do.
—an anonymous retort made after the trial of Jean Gianini

Lida Beecher was a young and beautiful schoolteacher in the small town of Poland, New York, a picturesque town in the midst of the Mohawk Valley. Poland is a place where neighbors all know one another and assist with anything necessary, but it is not a place where murder happens, especially the brutal slaying of a young teacher. In this setting, in the early twentieth century, Lida Beecher became the first teacher in the United States to be murdered by her student (Jean Gianini), and the result was one of the most dramatic trials and utterly unbelievable outcomes in the history of the Mohawk Valley.

Jean came to the small town of Poland from New York City. His father thought it would be better to get his son out of the sordid influences of a big city and have him educated and cultured in the ways of small-town America. In Poland, New York, the elder Mr. Charles Gianini was certainly pleased with his choice, having commented several times on the beauty of the area and the honest and hardworking people. He quickly integrated himself and his family into the community. Jean was motherless, having started his life out in tragedy when his mother passed away when he was only a year old.

Lida Beecher. *Herkimer County Historical Society.*

Jean's mother, Sallie McVey, had been deemed a violent drunkard who suffered from melancholia and was placed in St. Ann's Home, East Ninetieth Street, New York City. She was committed when Jean was just a baby and would never come out of the institution alive. As Sallie's condition worsened, she was further committed to the sanitarium for the insane; she was placed under the care of the Sisters of Charity. She died only two weeks after being committed. It was stated that Sallie McVey was an astoundingly beautiful woman in appearance and spirit, having been a very cultured person. She was only twenty years old when she died, which was the exact same age as Lida at the time of her murder. Charles Gianini later revealed at the trial of his son that his children had never been told the truth of their mother's mental condition nor the details of her institutionalization and tragic demise. He was heartbroken at his children having to learn the truth about their mother.

When it came to the reality of the matter, Jean Gianini was a troubled and restless young man who yearned for a life of adventure, including wanting to take a trip to the Panama Canal construction. This boredom and indifference to the constraints of the classroom caused Jean to be a less-than-stellar student both academically and behaviorally. He had an advocate in Miss Lida Beecher; even though she had trouble in the classroom with the young man, she still chose to take his life path under her wing. Her caring nature toward Jean had her writing to appropriate schools in order to secure a positive direction for the troubled young man.

LIDA'S LETTER OF SUPPORT

The *New York Times* was given a letter by the father of Lida Beecher and published it in its April 1, 1914 edition to show the compassion and concern that Lida had for her former student. When one realizes what was to soon follow, it only heightens the outrage felt at the meaningless slaughter of a teacher doing her best to assist a troubled student. Miss Beecher's letter to George Junior Republic was as follows:

Dear Sirs & Madams,

I was very much impressed with the work done for and by the boys and girls of your republic when I was visiting with a group of Cortland Normal Girls three years ago. Have you room for another citizen, a boy of fifteen years? He is a good hearted boy, one of my pupils last year and one of my most interesting boys. His mother died when he was too young to remember and left his father with Jean, the boy, and an older sister to care for, in New York City. Jean's father married again. The boy's father finally thought it best to move up into the country here, but it, of course, seemed pretty dull for such city-bred children, and the girl returned to New York City.

The father thinks a lot of the boy and has tried to do what he could do for him. As I have said, Jean was one of my pupils last year. He dislikes school work. He got a working certificate with his father's consent and went to work in the mills four miles from here. He became restless. I don't know what the trouble was, but he drew $5 and started to go somewhere away from home. He went to Buffalo, New York, Philadelphia, Albany and Lyons, among other places, but he got no work. Finally he called upon some humane society. They found out who he was, and he was sent to the Catholic Reform School in Utica. On his return he did not like it here and had nothing in view. If he could get into some place like the George Junior Republic, where he received a little treatment as well as hard work, it would be fine for him. He responds to kindness very readily. He is not a bad boy by any means. He is simply unhappy at home, but is ambitious, and has other fine qualities that would develop if he only had a little guidance to show him that he really could amount to something if he chooses to.

I had a little talk with Jean to-night about the place. Jean seemed to be quite interested when I explained as well as I could what was expected of him. Would you please send circulars of your school, for I am pretty sure that Jean's father, who is well educated and wants to make something out of his only son, would be delighted.

LIDA L. BEECHER

THE CRIME

Jean Gianini was seventeen years old, a slightly built lad of five feet, six inches tall, 125 pounds and rather meek looking behind his glasses. He wasn't of the manner or appearance of a coldblooded murderer. It was a chilly afternoon on March 27, 1914, when Lida Beecher happened upon young Jean in the village, as she was fond of walking the town all by herself. He told her that he had wanted her to see the new house his father was building on the outskirts of town. Dozens of witnesses had come forward who had seen Jean walking with Lida through the village and out of the town. The boy was not insidious or conniving in his planning but was rather callous and blunt, even having bragged to his chum, Brainerd Wilt, the week before that he was going to take care of Miss Beecher—that he was going to murder her.

BRAINERD WILT'S SIGNED AFFIDAVIT

I have known young Gianini for about one year and a half. When he came out of St. Vincent's Protectorate he told me how he got pinched. Two weeks after I came out of the woods Jean began to tell me his troubles. Monday night we were going down to the Erwin Hotel. Jean said to me in substance: "Miss Beecher is coming to my place to see my father about taking me back to school. She doesn't know where I live and I'll get her up there." He asked me to go along and help him. I told him I wouldn't. About 7:30 o'clock Tuesday night Jean came into the barn while I was cleaning the horses. We talked about the horses first. Then he said that he wanted to break into the Union store and get the money in there. He said he would skip out with the money. Then, he asked me if I would go with him. Then I said, "No, I don't want to get into it." Then he asked if I had any tools for the job and I said no. After that he began to talk about the teacher and said that she did him dirt and sent him away from school. He said he was going to kill her when he got the chance. I said I wouldn't work it that way. Then he said to me, "Have you got a revolver or a gag?" and I told him no. After that he went away. I was not a particular friend of his. I guess he thought I was though.

(Signed) Brainerd Wilt

It wasn't until they were well away from the village that Lida began to get nervous and wanted to return. It was at this point, secluded and out of earshot of anyone in town, that Jean struck his teacher in the back of the head with a wrench, finished her earthly existence with a knife, dragged her off the road, piled brush on top of her lifeless body and made a mad dash for it, leaving behind glaring clues that a Cub Scout could solve with a Sherlock Holmes Jr. detective kit. It would be a farmer by the name of Fitch, accompanied by his son, Ernest, who would be the first to discover the grisly scene. They were delivering their milk to Poland and came over the crest of Buck Hill when they came upon a woman's umbrella, a broken hair comb and a piece of rope that looked like a bit of clothesline. It was the blood on the pure white snow that startled Mr. Fitch and caused him to look in the direction of the woods, where it looked like something had been dragged. This went through a barbed wire fence and ended at a clump of trees. There were boot prints all over the area of the drag marks.

Fitch found Lida's body five rods away, stuffed under some bushes with a pool of blood around her head. She was lying facedown. Fitch hesitated. He then reached and touched her body, which was as cold as the snow it lay in. He then took his son into Poland to notify the town undertaker, Mr. Arthur E. Sprague. Sprague then went out to the scene and discovered a piece of cloth on the barbed wire fence and a button that must have been ripped from the suspect, as neither matched the victim. Lida had at least fourteen slash wounds on her face, marring the young teacher's beauty.

With witnesses coming forward who had seen Jean walking out of town, plus Gianini's verbal threats that he'd made to friends, the authorities had Jean as a strong suspect, yet the lad was missing. Jean was known for truancy and running away. George Sweet found the young man in Newport walking along train tracks and called Constable Frank Newman to come pick Jean up. It was on the way back to Poland that Jean immediately confessed to Constable Newman in the car.

"You've got something beside skipping home staring you in the face now," said Constable Newman. "You've got a murder charge ahead of you."

Jean said in a cold retort, "Well, they can't give me more than ten years for it."

Constable Newman remained calm and answered, "That's a pretty long term." When the constable returned Jean to his home, they were met by Sheriff Stitt and Coroner Huyck, and they quickly discovered that the buttons on Jean's jacket, the one he was wearing when Newman picked him up, matched the button found on the scene. The piece of fabric found on

Jean Gianini. *Herkimer County Historical Society.*

the barbed wire fence was matched up with a pair of Jean's pants that had a rip. It was also found that the jacket had some blood splatter on it. Jean was placed under arrest and taken by train to the Herkimer County Jail, escorted by Sheriff Stitt and Deputy Wilson. He was placed in the exact cell that Chester Gillette had occupied for his murder of Grace Brown, for which Gillette was executed in the electric chair. The same fate awaited Jean Gianini if found guilty of first-degree murder. The electric chair age cutoff was fourteen years old, and with Jean being years above that, and along with Jean's confession and overwhelming evidence, a conviction and date with the electric chair were all but certain. The one thing that the law enforcement community didn't expect was the defense that Jean was an idiot, an imbecile, a person with neither the mental capacity nor intelligence quotient to understand the ramifications of his criminal and murderous actions. Mental health professionals were brought in to examine the lad to determine the validity of Charles Gianini's claim that his son was insane.

THE ALIENIST'S INTERVIEW WITH JEAN GIANINI

Dr. Charles F. MacDonald, an alienist (psychiatrist) who was famous for treating people with mental illnesses, walked into the cell at the Herkimer County Jail where Jean Gianini now sat for murdering his teacher, Miss Lida Beecher, in the small hamlet of Poland. The cell was small and cold, and the jailers were kind enough to allow the doctor to bring in a chair so that he might sit and converse with the young lad. What transpired stunned the alienist, who wrote down the answers from the remorseless murderer. The doctor had waited some time before his visit to give Jean time to think about his actions. What follows was taken from Dr. MacDonald's notes of his interview with Jean Gianini and published in the Tuesday, May 19, 1914 edition of the *Syracuse Journal*:

"Sure I killed her," declared Jean in an arrogant tone. "I aint ashamed of it. She snitched on me and the old man walloped me. The other kids never got a lickin'. I always got along all right with the other teachers but Miss Beecher snitched on me every chance she got. She would have me arrested too, and I knew it so I killed her. I had my revenge and that is all there is to it."

The alienist pushed forward in his chair and leaned in closer, looking over the top rim of his eye glasses and asked, "Did you think you were justified in doing such a deed?"

"Sure," replied Jean full of pride and boasting. "I know enough about her and the way she treated me. I aint afraid of what I done." Jean then laughed, covering his mouth with the back of his hand.

"You seem pretty cheerful about it."

"Why shouldn't I be," replied Jean with a smirk. "It's all over and I might as well be as glad as I can."

The alienist then leaned back and talked in a softer tone, asking Jean, "You are not at all sorry for what you have done?"

"I don't feel sorry about anything only that it's got me in all this trouble."

Dr. MacDonald stopped his scribing and spoke looking the young man straight in the eye and asked, "Would you do it over again?"

"I can't do it again!" snapped Jean with instant anger. "It's done already!"

This only bolstered Dr. MacDonald's resolve who then pushed Jean into a shocking confession, "Well, if Miss Beecher was alive would you do it?"

Jean crossed his arms, smiled really wide and answered the doctor with a cocky, "Sure."

"Do you know the penalty for murder?"

"Why yes. I can get the chair if I am found guilty in the 3rd degree or get life in prison if they get me for 2nd degree."

"How about the 1st degree?"

"I don't know anything about that," snapped Jean.

"You would be sent to the electric chair," replied the alienist. "Do you know what that means?"

"Sure I do," replied Jean. "But I aint afraid of the chair. I aint a-goin' to be afraid of nothing. Of course I'd rather go to prison than to the chair but I ain't afraid. I done it and that's all there is to it."

Dr. MacDonald went on to conclude that Jean Gianini was "absolutely devoid of sentiment, feeling or regret" for his horrible deed. Dr. MacDonald testified in the Herkimer County Courthouse that he had thoroughly examined Jean Gianini both mentally and physically, including several recognized tests for mental deficiency. He determined that the boy had a small head and that it was longer in length than in width. The doctor went on to say that the arch of the pallet was high and narrow, a condition often found in idiots and imbeciles, and said that the boy's left and right face were not equal. These features, Dr. MacDonald testified, are characteristics of some of the stigmata of degenerates. He stated that the angles of the ears on the head were also noted as odd and that Jean had tremor of the hands. "In my opinion, Jean Gianini is suffering from a condition of mental weakness known as imbecility," stated Dr. MacDonald.

LIDA'S FATHER VISITS JEAN GIANINI IN JAIL

Reverend W.A. Beecher came from his town of Sennett to visit the accused sixteen-year-old murderer of his daughter at the Herkimer County Jail on a brisk spring day on March 30. The kindhearted reverend, who was gentle of spirit, had come to pick up the body of his daughter and decided to visit Jean and speak to him of the crime to acquire further details on the murder. The reverend sheepishly stepped into the jail cell and shook the boy's hand. The jailers reported that Reverend Beecher showed no malice or anger toward Jean and, if anything, was empathetic and sorrowful toward the lad. The reverend was interested in how Jean had led his daughter to the place of her death and what his exact motive was for the dastardly deed. The reverend's voice was described as serene and not high in tone or anger but rather gentle and low.

The reverend asked Jean outright how he had seduced his daughter to her demise. Jean answered:

> *I met her on the street and asked her if she'd like to go and see the new house my father was building. I told her she could talk to my father about getting me back into school. I told her the new house my father was building was outside the village. This was a lie. We walked out of Poland and we walked quite a ways before she got scared and wanted*

to go back. She turned and started back so I took the iron wrench I had in my pocket and stepped behind her and struck her in the back of the head. She fell to the ground and was screaming so I took out my knife and I slashed her.

During this exchange, Reverend Beecher sat across from Jean and continued to hold the young man's hand. "I dragged her into the bushes," Jean said as he went on describing in cold detail and limited emotion what he had done.

Reverend Beecher, his voice choked with emotion, said to his daughter's murderer, "Goodbye, Jean. Now, Miss Beecher would want you to repent and be a good boy. I cherish no revengeful feeling towards you, but I do want you to be a good boy and repent." The jailers stated that from his reaction, Reverend Beecher did not believe that Jean was a sane boy. The reverend went to visit Charles Gianini, Jean's father, to offer his sympathy and consolation.

"I cannot believe my son is guilty," lamented Charles. "But if he is I'd rather be in your place than mine." Reverend Beecher traveled back to Poland, where his daughter's autopsy had been completed and where he held a religious service with a packed church filled with residents of Poland. Reverend Beecher then took his daughter's body back to his hometown of Sennett, where Lida was to be buried.

THE TRIAL OF JEAN GIANINI

The Herkimer County Courthouse was the location of the dramatic trial. Lida Beecher had come to Poland, New York, fresh from the Cortland, New York Normal School in 1913 and would never make a career out of improving the minds of the young. Instead, her murder halted a promising life and sent two families and a community into a turmoil that reached its apex at the trial. The proceedings were overseen by Justice Devendorf, with the prosecution's case delivered by District Attorney Farrell and Special Prosecutor Charles D. Thomas. Thomas first called to the stand Mr. Ernest Fitch, who came upon the body of Miss Beecher. He also displayed the wrench and the knife that had been used in the murder. Other physical evidence included the button and cloth found at the scene that matched Jean's clothing, as well as the bloody shirt. This was followed by a series of witnesses who testified that Jean had talked before the crime about hurting Miss Beecher.

Lawrence Lamb was first and described that weeks before the crime, while in conversation, Jean had stated to him that "I may some day put an end to Miss Beecher." Next up was Leo Coonradt, another young man and acquaintance of Jean, who had been told by the defendant, "I'll do something to Miss Beecher the people of Poland will not forget." The last of these witnesses was James Brothers, who stated that Jean said that he was going to get even with Miss Beecher. The undertaker, Sprague, was then called to the stand to testify to the state of Lida's body and the scene. These gruesome details stunned the courtroom. The star witness who was called by Special Prosecutor Thomas was Constable Frank Newman, a well-respected and admired lawman who had garnered the confession from the young man. It seemed that Jean's guilt was a mere technicality and that his date with the electric chair would be put in stone, and rather quickly.

It was the defense's case of insanity that might be the only thing to keep the lad from frying. The defense attorneys, John F. McIntyre and David G. Hirsch, were from New York City and had to prove that Jean Gianini was indeed insane. The first person to be called was Jean's father, Charles Gianini, who would have to testify on the mental condition and drunkenness of Jean's mother. Justice Devendorf requested that all women leave the courtroom for this part of the testimony. It was the first time that Jean heard of the tragic drinking of his mother, her committal to the mental hospital and her tragic death.

Next up on the stand was Dr. Charles Weeks of New York City, who testified that he was the attending physician at Jean's birth and that he had helped treat Jean's mother's alcoholism. After Charles's and Dr. Week's testimony, the women were allowed back into the courtroom, including Jean's sister, Catherine, who hadn't seen her brother in years. Catherine was described as a beautiful and elegant woman who held herself to the proper decorum and spent the remainder of the trial weeping softly into her white handkerchief. At this point, the courtroom was filled with spectators from the field of mental health, including Dr. C.F. Wagner, superintendent of the Binghamton State Hospital for the Mentally Insane.

The next witness for the defense was Dr. Hersey G. Locke from Herkimer, New York, who was a well-known and highly respected psychopathy expert. Dr. Locke went on to testify that Jean was a low-

The Gianini jury. *Front row, left to right*: Warren W. Fenton, Mohawk; Webster Rasbach, Herkimer; Homer Nicholas, Norway; George Hamrighaus, Salisbury; A. Jordan, Herkimer; and Bronson Plather, Frankfort. *Second row*: Joseph Frinkle, Cold Brook; Terrance O'Day, Herkimer; Luke Byrnes, West Winfield; and Edward J. Turney, Columbia. *Third row*: Henry Staley, Dolgeville; and Seward G. Bellinger, Danube. *Back row*: Court Officer William Syllaboch, Sheriff William Stitt and Court Officer Ross Sadler. *Herkimer County Historical Society.*

grade imbecile and that because of this, he should not be found guilty of his deeds. The doctor went on to state that Jean should have been institutionalized many years earlier and that the young man belonged among other feebleminded people. Dr. Locke went on to testify that Jean had no restraint in him and that because of this, he was paranoid, delusional, angry and resentful. This mania, in people like Jean, could result, according to Dr. Locke, in cruelty toward animals and children. Dr. Locke then stated that people of this nature will assault and murder to take out their personal demons and create internal satisfaction. Dr. Locke felt that Jean should be institutionalized and not placed in the electric chair.

The defense called Dr. Charles MacDonald, the acclaimed alienist, who went into great detail about his jailhouse interview with Jean. At this point, Special Prosecutor Thomas rattled Dr. MacDonald, causing the physician to lose his temper and snap a few times as the prosecution went after the insanity defense. It was the testimony of Dr. Henry H. Goddard, superintendent of the State Training School for the Feeble Minded at

Vineland, New Jersey, who would prove most difficult for the prosecution to diffuse. Dr. Goddard testified that Jean had the mental capacity of a ten-year-old and that he had an abnormal sense of situations. He testified that in his medical opinion Jean Gianini was an imbecile. Dr. Goddard maintained his professional composure and did not yield moral ground to Special Prosecutor Thomas as he was cross-examined. All the alienists had to do was convince the twelve men on the jury of Jean's insanity.

THE STUNNING VERDICT

The case was concluded and handed over to the jury, with District Attorney Farrell refusing to speculate on the outcome. It was not out of the realm of possibility that the members of the prosecution would feel that they had their man ready to fry for his murderous deed. Throughout the entire trial, Jean appeared restless and bored, many times placing his chin in his hand. Thousands of spectators lined up on the street outside the courtroom waiting to hear the verdict. It took twenty hours of deliberations before the jurors returned to the packed courtroom and delivered the most stunning verdict in the history of criminal proceedings in the Mohawk Valley: not guilty by reason of insanity. Jean Gianini would be committed to the Matteawan Asylum for the Criminally Insane. Both sides of the courtroom gasped at the result.

The jury came under intense public scrutiny and outrage, for the chair had seemed a foregone conclusion. The defense attorneys told Jean not to smile as he was escorted from the courtroom through a stunned crowd. It was said that "even God Almighty don't know what a jury will do." It was felt by many that the jurors had been duped by a smart defense lawyer. Jean had admittedly planned and killed Miss Lida Beecher and would serve no jail time for his crime nor travel to Auburn for a date with the electric chair. Lida's father, Reverend Beecher, declared his disappointment and regretted the lack of justice for his daughter. The crime and result shattered the Beecher family, who lost a young, beautiful and promising daughter, as well as the Gianinis, whose son and brother would be committed to an asylum. As Jean was taken from his cell, he left behind writing that was said to be too vulgar to be printed; however, one poem was printed in the Thursday, June 11, 1914 edition of the *Journal and Republican* of Lowville, New York:

My name is Gianini I would have you know.
And I always have trouble wherever I go.
To be thought a tough it is my delight.
And I'm thinking and planning both day and night.
I killed Lida Beecher with an old monkey wrench.
And they took me before the judge on the bench.
The sentence they gave me it caused me to smile.
It was "He is not guilty he's an imbecile."
Now here is thanks to the jurors who let me go free.
The foolishest men I ever did see.
When they came marching in it raised up my hair.
I thought sure they'd say "He must sit in the chair."
Now, soon I must leave you and bid you adieu.
And the dollars I've cost you won't be a few.
I never will fear if I can find McIntyre.
For I really believe he could save me from hell-fire.

A Lecture to the Ladies

This city is darkened by the foul crime of scandal, even more than by the black
clouds of smoke that hang over it and shut out the light of the day.
—*Father Angelo, St. Patrick's Church, Utica, New York, 1916*

UTICA, NEW YORK, APRIL 1916

The sermon that Father Angelo delivered to his congregation condemned sin
put forth by women, especially those who keep company with what the priest
referred to as "Mrs. Scandal," which had a disastrous effect on a community
and destroyed the body and the soul. His mission service at St. Patrick's
Church in Utica had row after row of women, at whom he pointed and
directed his sermon, blaming the lure of the scandal as dangerous to a city
and community. The *Utica Herald-Dispatch* described his lecture as dignified
yet critical of the sinful women in attendance. He stood in his starched frock,
looking down upon the gathered women and saying, "My subject tonight
of fear will fail to please you. I am going to speak of the greatest mischief
maker in the parish. Not only that but I shall mention her name. I wonder
where is she tonight?"

The ladies in the pews craned their necks to see if somebody else was the
victim of Father Angelo's wrath. He continued, "Is she perhaps in some
moving picture show? Is she perhaps in some public dance hall? Is she perhaps
in some theater? Is she perhaps walking down Genesee Street attracting the
attention of men? Where is she?" Father Angelo's words echoed throughout

the church and kept the ladies in attendance enthralled as he gripped the podium with white-knuckled fury. Each woman wanted it to be the person beside her and not herself. "Is she in the temple of God? She is everywhere. Do you know her name, this woman that I speak of?" Then he went on to give her name. "Listen, I shall tell you. Her name is 'Mrs. Scandal' or 'Mrs. Bad Example.' Is not scandal the excuse of the defrauder, the defense of the libertine, the apology of the drunkard, the plea of the negligent Catholic, the reason of the grafter? The vice of the scandal is one of the insidious vices of the age. It falls upon greedy ears and finds a ready market. Woe to the world because of scandal."

At this point, Father Angelo paused for dramatic effect, with all womanly ears pricked up to see if he would name specific people of the parish, none wanting it to be her. He took a deep breath with his eyes closed, opened them to the rows of pews and started again:

> *Between the sin of scandal and other sins there exists this difference. The latter sins kill the soul of him alone who commits them, whilst scandal, besides affecting the perpetrator, causes the eternal ruin of the neighbor. It is a great evil for a rich man to lose his wealth, a just man to be deprived of his good name, a happy man to be murdered, a prosperous country to be stricken with famine, a contending kingdom to be betrayed into the hands of the enemy, but the evil of scandal is even more enormous and deplorable for the reason that theft and calumny and murder and famine and treason deprive us of the goods of nature only, but scandal deprives of the good of grace. The one robs us of temporal, the other of eternal goods.*

At this point, Father Angelo dialed down the inflection of his voice; however, it didn't affect the delivery or message:

> *Theologians teach that the extent of an injury done the neighbor is the rule by which to measure the guilt consequent to the act. Now, if he who takes from his neighbor temporal goods is guilty of a glaring act of injustice, is not he who deprives him of eternal goods? If it is a terrible crime to kill the body, what must it be to kill the soul? Christ says, "Fear ye not them that kill the body and are not able to kill the soul, but rather fear him, that can destroy both body and soul into hell." Such a one is he who gives scandal because he causes both body and soul to be put in hell.*

Now it was time for Father Angelo to direct his strict point at the sinful women in his congregation:

Guilt of this crime are mothers who curse and quarrel and drink to excess in the presence of their children. Guilty of this crime are mothers who do not raise their children in the Catholic faith, and correct their faults. Guilty of this crime are mothers who allow their sons and daughters to associate with bad companies. Guilty of this crime are mothers who permit their daughters to keep company to all hours of the night and to dress in gaudy and scandalous faults. Guilty of this crime are mothers who consult fashion plates oftener than the Holy Bible. Guilty of this crime are mothers who attach more importance to their jewelry and their dresses rather than religious obligations. Guilty of this crime are mothers who do not send their children to church on Sundays. Woe to the world because of scandal.

Father Angelo's degradation of the women did not end yet. He continued on with his sermon:

There is no crime more rife than scandal which is given and taken at all times in all places and by everyone. Who is the young girl that refrains from giving scandal? Not the girl who spends more time in front of the mirror than in prayer. Not the girl who thinks more of her picture than her religious duties. Not the girl who adorns her head with heaps of elegant false hair trying to make herself more beautiful than she really is. Not the girl who goes indiscriminately to all sorts of dance halls, theaters, moving picture shows, and places of amusement, in reading pernicious literature and identifies herself with the heroine in the novel and takes her actions for the rule in her life. Not the girl who goes to church on Sunday morning rather to display her showy dress than to assist in the holy sacrifice of the mass. Not the girl who seldom goes to confession. Woe the world because of scandal.

Another dramatic pause occurred as Father Angelo stopped to catch his breath, sweeping back a few fallen strands of his wispy gray hair. He grasped the pulpit and continued his lecture to the congregation:

Who is the woman that refrains from giving scandal? Not the new woman that neglects her home duties to emphasize to the world at large woman's rights. Not the childless woman the sumptuously gowned or well fed, delicately reared dame who scorns the labor of bringing up little children.

Not the worldly woman who is money mad, and clothes mad, and hungers and thirsts after the limelight. Not the ambitious woman who lusts for wealth and sells her daughter into marriage to a rich society man, the highest bidder whose yachts and automobiles and opera boxes will afford her ample opportunities for social exploitations. Not the unfaithful woman who furnishes grist for the divorce mills and for the scandal factories. Such a woman does not refrain from giving scandal. Woe to the world because of scandal.

With his sermon reaching its apex, Father Angelo hit his last wind of condemnation:

This city is darkened by the crime of scandal, even more than by the black clouds of smoke that hang over us and shut out the light of the day. Doubters there are here young girls whose earliest memories have been associated with drunkenness and debauchery, young women who have been driven to infamy and despair by the shameful conduct of their parents, aged mothers who have seen all their love and self-sacrifice turned into bitterness and despair by the saloon, the gambling den, the dance halls and houses of infamy. Every day we meet women who enter the church to pray then leave and gossip about their neighbor. Every day we meet women who pray for us to forgive their trespasses yet they never forgive or forget an injury but rather knife and destroy the reputation of their neighbor. We shudder with terror at the horrors of the European war. A battlefield of human slaughter. Trenches of hell yet women will continue their scandalous ways.

Father Angelo would not go on to assist in the woman's rights movement. He would not go on to support the equal rights amendment. Meanwhile, crimes continued to be committed throughout the Mohawk Valley.

Lumberjack Fugitive

Please let me say goodbye to my sickly sister.
—Freeman Borst pleading with lawmen
before he bolted from his sister's room and went on the lam

Schoharie, New York, 1921

If one were to believe that there is such a thing as an evil seed, you'd certainly nominate Freeman Borst to wear the crown as king of the insidious. The large and powerful lumberjack had stolen property, robbed innocent citizens, terrorized women and assaulted young girls in three states. He had decades of criminality and recidivism along with cowardly runs from the law and a multiplicity of dramatic prison escapes. If Borst was indeed born bad, it ran in his criminal family, with his two brothers being in jail serving life sentences for murder. The documentation of his crimes goes back on findable records to 1910, when he was arrested in Oneonta, New York, for grand larceny in the first degree when he impersonated a police officer and robbed an innocent farmer who had been visiting. Borst had approached Edward Saumier at the train station and declared that he was an officer of the law and told Mr. Saumier that he was to pay him a fine right then and there for certain transgressions. When Mr. Saumier refused, Borst put his hands in the man's pockets and took his only money, in the sum of four dollars. Borst also made the man give him his watch that had been valued at fourteen dollars. It had been reported that Freeman Borst had also previously served a jail term of seven years at Dannemora State Prison for assault. The lumberjack had even once tried a new occupation as a barber.

Freeman Borst couldn't contain the criminal demons that festered within him, as he was arrested and jailed in Fonda in 1916 for larceny and burglary. He escaped the prison and moved his sins to Boston, Massachusetts, and Bridgeport, Connecticut, where he was arrested in each and escaped from both jails. His jail-breaking skills put him on the "most wanted" lists, but it was the next series of crimes that caused him to reach the apex of his lawbreaking. The native of Sharon Springs went on to criminally assault a seven-year-old girl and commit carnal abuse of a three-year-old girl. He was on the loose and considered extremely dangerous, and law enforcement throughout New York State was on alert. In Oneonta, Borst was arrested for assaulting another young girl and then escaped that jail. He was on the run and had relatives in the area. When police officers tracked him to his sister's house, he pleaded to go into the other room. "Please let me say goodbye to my sickly sister," he requested. The kindhearted lawmen agreed, and Borst bolted from the house and fled into the thick nearby woods. A rather large posse was gathered, along with a sizeable pack of bloodhounds that were quickly on the scent. Evil scum leave a rather distinct scent trail. They tracked Borst to another house, whereupon he bolted from the porch and dashed back into the woods. The search went into the night, becoming futile as Freeman Borst, the "Lumberjack Fugitive," had once again escaped.

It was smart police work by Sheriff Converse of Otsego County that led to Borst's capture. While the sheriff was talking with new prisoners of the Otsego County Jail, two men recently captured identified a rendering of Freeman Borst yet told the sheriff that this person was going by the name of Frank Brownell. These men said that they had recently gotten out of Monroe County Penitentiary, where they were cellmates with Brownell, who closely resembled Borst. Sheriff Converse called the warden where Brownell was being held and discovered that the man was soon to be released. The sheriff sent Undersheriff Rose out to pick up the man, if he was indeed Borst. Being arrested and jailed numerous times, Borst could not hide under his criminal alias, Frank Brownell, as Undersheriff Rose quickly recognized and arrested the Lumberjack Fugitive. It was under heavy guard and thick shackles that the most dangerous fugitive in New York State was brought back to Cooperstown, New York, where he was turned over to Schoharie County authorities. The police mentioned that Borst was married yet nobody could locate the man's wife, as she had disappeared. The nightmare of Freeman Borst had come to an end, yet the details of his final days are unknown. The Lumberjack Fugitive, like most vicious scumbags, never specifically died; he just faded away into the mists of oblivion.

Killed in the Bootleg War

Two cars full of professional killers blocked their path both forward and
backwards so they couldn't get out. They were finished.
—*law enforcement officers at their re-creation of the murder of the Malkoons*

FRANKFORT, NEW YORK, 1930

The police discovered the bodies lying in the middle of a back dirt road
riddled with bullets—authorities determined that it had all the earmarks of a
crime syndicate hit. The police identified the men as the father and son team
of Louis, fifty-four, and Rocco Malkoon, twenty-three, who together operated
a still. With the onset of the prohibition amendment to the Constitution in
1919 that made alcohol illegal in the United States, stills and bootlegging
ran rampant in many cities, including Utica, New York, a city that had Irish,
Italian, Polish and German immigrants whose entire cultures revolved around
wine and beer for dinner and with most being able to make their own. It
was determined that there had been at least twenty stills operating in Utica
alone, not to mention the dozens located in the surrounding foothills. The
well-meaning law did nothing but create more problems for law enforcement,
with bribes, bootlegging, turf wars and murders resulting.

The Malkoons' murders would have been nothing unusual in the country,
let alone Utica, New York. A decade before the death of the Malkoons,
Utica was embroiled in what was referred to as the "whiskey scandal," when
train employees were searching passengers coming into Utica. They would

Louis and Rocco Malkoon. *Oneida County Historical Society.*

search the persons, rifle through their luggage and seize any alcohol found for personal consumption or reselling. If passengers refused, civilians dressed as policemen would come forward and force them to open their liquor-laden suitcases. Federal investigators came to Utica and stormed Union Station based on the complaints of those who had thousands of dollars of liquor seized by the railroad employees and their fake policemen.

It was September 26, 1930, when the police authorities found the bodies of Louis and Rocco Malkoon dead and filled with lead on the Lonely Jones Road just outside Frankfort, New York, in Herkimer County. Police theorized by reviewing the scene that the Malkoons had been murdered because they were lowering the price they were charging for alcohol, thus challenging the viability of the business of rival still operators. Police theorized that the father and son had been lured to the rural location by rivals wanting to discuss a partnership in the illegal liquor business. Once the Malkoons drove down this road, their fate was sealed—police re-creating the scene stated that "two cars full of professional killers blocked their path both forward and backwards so they couldn't get out. They were finished."

The bodies of Louis and Rocco were filled with .45-caliber bullets and peppered thoroughly with pellet shot from multiple shotguns. It was overkill, meant to send a message to other still operators in the Mohawk Valley. The next day, police hauled the Malkoons' still partner, Paolo Basile, into headquarters to be grilled on what he knew about the murders. Basile was an

Italian immigrant who had come to Utica from Italy in 1919, leaving behind a wife and child. Basile was well known as a master maker and top-notch repairer of stills. He was a tinsmith by trade and was extremely handy to the illegal still operators. It was said that they would visit Basile's apartment at all hours of the day and night, picking him up to repair or build stills all over the Mohawk Valley. These men would rap on his window so as to not bring suspicion or disturb the other occupants of the apartment building.

Basile did not cooperate with police and told them that he had no information on who had killed his partners; he also refused to provide the names of anybody who operated a still. Days later, Basile disappeared, and police figured that he went back to Italy, for his bank account had been closed and his apartment appeared to have been abandoned. Police officers located and confiscated the Malkoons' still, operated in New York Mills, New York. They also discovered that the Malkoons and Basile owed a local businessman $1,000 for sugar. Police also found proof that Basile had recently been paid $1,000 to build a still in Utica but lost the money in a card game and neither built the still nor returned the money. Within days, Basile's body was found floating in the Barge Canal in Utica with a sash cord wound tightly around his neck. Police theorized that he had been killed because he truly knew who had killed the Malkoons. "The man simply knew too much," said lawmen. It was theorized that the still operators feared that the man would squeal on them and their profitable liquor business.

The Dastardly Abortion Case

I will be here 7 to 9am, 12 to 3:30pm and 6:30 to 8:30pm.
Drop a note under the door (signed) Bert Peck.
—*sign on the door letting women know when they could come and get an abortion*

GLOVERSVILLE, NEW YORK, 1930

On April 19, 1930, Dr. Woodard Shaw and Dr. M.F. Donnelly rushed to the Gloversville home of Mrs. Ruth Leverdure, as it was reported that the woman was in dire need of medical attention. Upon inspection of the gravely ill woman, the doctors determined that she needed to be transported to the hospital. The two medical professionals were in shock. Her condition, in their opinion, was caused from an attempted abortion. The resulting case shook Gloversville, a small-town manufacturing community, to the roots of its moral base.

In the midst of Fulton County, in the hamlet of Gloversville, New York, there occurred back on April 17, 1930, a criminal case that would prove to be dramatic and horrific to the entire community—Bert Peck stood accused of performing an illegal abortion. At the time, Gloversville was the largest area in the United States for the manufacturing of gloves. When this dastardly crime occurred, 90 percent of gloves sold in the United States were being manufactured in Gloversville. The nearby forests that provided ample bark for tanning is what had led to the region's industrial exclusivity. It didn't help Mr. Peck that the area had been settled by Puritans at the end of the eighteenth century who lived and breathed high moral and religious standards. On top of that, abortion was against the law. But to commit such a heinous crime in a blue-collar, Puritan town was more than the upstanding citizenry of Gloversville could handle.

Dr. Shaw and Dr. Donnelly informed the Gloversville Police Department of the partial abortion procedure done on the woman, and they, in turn, sent police officers, District Attorney Bernard W. Kearney and Assistant District Attorney Willard L. Best to the bedside of Mrs. Leverdure to question her. She stated in her bedside affidavit that she had indeed been pregnant and had gone with her friend Marjorie Cassare to 2 South School Street on April 17, 1930, and paid Bert Peck twenty-five dollars to conduct an abortion of her unborn child.

Based on Mrs. Leverdure's bedside affidavit, police officers conducted a raid on the residence of Bert Peck. Motorcycle Policeman Brothers was the first law officer on the scene, and the sign he saw on the door alarmed him: "I will be here 7 to 9am, 12 to 3:30pm and 6:30 to 8:30pm. Drop a note under the door (signed) Bert Peck." Officer Brothers removed the sign, which would be used as evidence in the court case. The most offensive items were waiting for him and other officers inside Peck's apartment. The police officers entered the residence and were shocked to discover all sorts of instruments, equipment, bandages and medicaments for the sole purpose of committing illegal abortions. Bert Peck was then placed under arrest and housed in the Fulton County Jail. His bail was set at $2,500, which was an astounding amount of money in 1930, yet two citizens stepped up and bailed him out.

The incident shocked the entire Gloversville township, with citizens up in arms over someone other than a doctor performing such procedures right in their midst. The Fulton County Grand Jury deemed that there was enough evidence to conduct a trial by peer. A jury composed of twelve men was selected, and the trial began in February 1931. Bert Peck's defense attorneys, Harold W. Ward and Harry F. Dunkel, petitioned the court to have the case dismissed since the memories of Ruth Leverdure and Marjorie Cassare were vague on Peck's description. They stated that the wrong man was being accused; however, District Attorney Kearney revealed a sworn statement by Mrs. Cassare that Peck's former apartment was the precise location of the procedure. Kearney had taken Mrs. Cassare, her husband and Gloversville police chief George R. Smith to the apartment, which they walked through, and Mrs. Cassare signed the statement right at that time.

The courtroom was packed with Gloversville residents anxious to see justice delivered to Bert Peck. The graphic details were shocking to the upstanding citizens. Judge Calderwood concluded by apologizing to the jury and those in attendance, for he claimed that it had been the most unpleasant trial he had overseen since being elected judge. Peck decided to not testify in his defense and had to sit while the prosecution brought out the instruments of his profitable and illegal medical procedures. Dr. Woodard Shaw, Dr. M.F. Donnelly and Dr. H.G. McKillip testified and described the way the procedure was done and how Mrs. Laverdure's baby had been partially left inside her womb. The defense rested, and the judge sent the jury to chambers at 4:10 p.m. At 8:35 p.m., the jury returned. The courtroom became silent as the foreman stood up and delivered a guilty verdict. Bert Peck received four to eight years in a New York State prison for his dastardly crime.

The Creeping Death

Wet Brain.
—moniker given by law officers as the reason for a fatality
via the Creeping Death

Gloversville, New York, 1935

The man had purchased the still-made alcoholic bottled spirit and admired
the sweet smell of the beverage before he gulped it down. Little did he
know that he was drinking bottled poison. His life would soon be over, and
he would be yet another victim of what local law officials were referring to
as the "Creeping Death." When all was said and done, fifteen people in the
Gloversville area and eighteen more through to Utica, New York, a total
of thirty-three victims, met an extremely painful death by poison from
illegally made booze. It was a death that crept up on them, with victims
knowing that they were about to die and with doctors not being able to do
anything about it.

Buying and selling alcohol had been declared illegal by the United States
government with the approval of the Eighteenth Amendment, creating
a prohibition that lasted from 1920 until 1933. All this amendment did
was create an increased demand for alcohol and spur the creation of
speakeasies, backwoods stills, rumrunners, bootleggers and a vast array of
organized crime to satisfy the masses wanting to partake in a tasty illegal
beverage. Even after the repeal, it was difficult for many still operators and

those who mixed their own booze to give up the lucrative business and go legit. The repeal of prohibition had outlawed the still manufacturing of spirits without a license.

It was January 1935, and the cold wind was coming down the Adirondack Mountains, crunchy snow was blanketing the Mohawk Valley and death followed. Police authorities knew right away that they had an epidemic of poisoned illegal alcohol, as dozens of people died within a one-week period. Their suspicions were confirmed by the autopsies that opened up the stomachs of the victims, revealing a pungent odor of alcohol that came from a massive amount of lethal rubbing alcohol, the bookend of the evidence being the massive leakage of fluid from the brain—bringing about the name "wet brain." The lawmen in Gloversville coined the epidemic the "Creeping Death." Doctors explained that those blinded by alcohol poisoning would never regain their vision but could live if the contents were pumped from their stomachs. Several victims of the Creeping Death survived, to doctors' amazement, but it was discovered that they had swallowed very little of the poison, thus keeping their brains from oozing and delaying their dates with the Grim Reaper.

The big break in the case came quickly when Gloversville detective Harry Hart rushed to the bedside of the dying Mrs. Lena Snyder. The woman was distraught and in severe pain as the doctors pumped what they could from her stomach but essentially told her that there was nothing more they could do; they left her to die in her bed. At least she would get justice for herself and the other victims: she told Detective Hart that she had purchased a pint of alcohol for one dollar from Mrs. Mary Derrico of Gloversville. After this revelation, police authorities scrambled to arrest Mrs. Derrico to try to stop the deaths. Mrs. Derrico was arrested, as was her son, Thomas Derrico, as authorities seized a pint of the tainted alcohol from her residence. The mother and son cooperated with authorities and revealed that they had purchased three five-gallon tins of the alcohol from John DiPedro and Salvatore DiDominick, both of Little Falls, New York. Mrs. Derrico also revealed some possible stores that were selling the illegally made alcohol. The extent of the people dying from the illegal alcohol made it all the way to Washington, D.C., where the Alcohol Tax Unit of the Treasury Department scrambled manpower to conduct raids throughout Gloversville and Fulton County in conjunction with District Attorney Bernard W. Kearney.

Law authorities, led by Investigative Supervisor Guy Stowell of Oppenheim, swept in and arrested DiPedro and DiDominick, and they brought the four in to appear in front of Supreme Court justice Erskine C. Rogers. Mrs. Mary

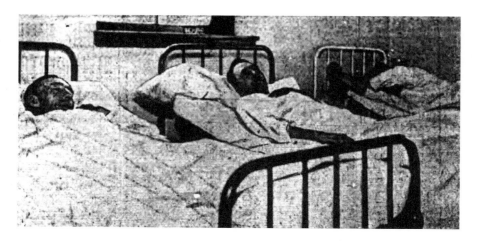

Three victims of the Creeping Death recover in the hospital. They would be the lucky few to survive drinking the deadly concoction. *From the* Gloversville and Johnstown [*New York*] Morning Herald.

Derrico, who spoke little English, had to use her son as her interpreter. She was charged with the sale of illegal alcohol and manslaughter in the second degree in the death of Lena Snyder. Thomas Derrico was charged with the sale of illegal alcohol. DiDominick was not charged and was released due to lack of evidence, but DiPedro was charged with the illegal sale of alcohol and second-degree manslaughter. DiPedro cooperated with authorities and led them to a house in Utica, New York, where he claimed to have purchased the barrels of alcohol from Salvatore DiBenedetto and his two sons, Michael and Phillip. Police authorities and U.S. Treasury officials surrounded the DiBenedetto home, fearing that they would be desperate men, not wanting to go easily into custody. The arrests were made without drama, and the authorities found in the home an entire alcoholic beverage–making arsenal, including wine, malt, hops, wooden vats, empty bottles, fittings, valves and pipes, yet the tins of poisonous alcohol were nowhere to be found.

Besides Mrs. Lena Snyder, some of the dead included Luther Benedict, Bert Grant, Charles Bates and Merill Dence, along with twenty-eight other victims. Treasury officials swept through more than twenty-eight stores throughout Fulton County, with District Attorney Kearney declaring, "It is practically impossible to make a purchase of illegal liquor now. We will continue to make raids."

In the midst of all this tragedy and law movements, a thirty-five-year career lawman with an impeccable record came under attack via vicious rumors.

Gloversville police chief George Smith suffered public humiliation as rumors spread throughout Gloversville High School that the police chief had been taking protection money from Mary Derrico to look the other way regarding her illegal business. The gossip spread to the community. Throughout the Mohawk Valley, small towns and little cities like Gloversville are very close-knit communities, with everybody knowing everybody. The chief knew that Anthony Derrico was attending the Gloversville High School, yet when he asked the lad if he had started the rumors, the teenager denied it. The chief needed to end the unnecessary sideshow, so he obtained signed affidavits from Mary and Thomas Derrico that he never gave them protection money. The police chief issued this challenge: "I have been a member of the police department for thirty-five years and am not afraid of inspection of my record. I have never taken a penny worth of bribes or graft, and I will be glad to face the persons who dare say so. Come forward, anyone; if you have proof, place it in front of the police committee or common council. It cuts me deeply to be the target of insidious rumors. I have been strict in the performance of my duties in all my years of wearing the badge."

ACTIVE IN POISON LIQUOR PROBE HERE

Evidence in liquor deaths: Gloversville chief of police George R. Smith (left) and Sergeant Bernard Murphy inspect bottles of the deadly beverage. Also pictured is a bottle, with the label indicating that it came from Mary Derrico's place. *From the* Gloversville and Johnstown [*New York*] Morning Herald.

In Fulton County, Mary Derrico had trouble attending the trial and hearings, as she was sixty years old and had a fragile heart. This didn't impede justice, as she and Thomas pleaded guilty to selling alcohol illegally in violation of the Alcoholic Beverage Control Law, and both were fined $200 each by Judge F. Law Comstock. Mrs. Derrico was still being charged with second-degree manslaughter and remained out on her $20,000 bail. Upon hearing that she was still being charged in the death of Lena Snyder, Mrs. Derrico became emotional, wailing as she placed her face into her hands. She sobbed until her son calmed her down. Thomas paid the fine and escorted his mother out of the courtroom.

At a later date, John DiPedro of Little Falls had his manslaughter charge dropped when he pleaded guilty to the illegal transportation of alcohol and was fined $100 by Judge T. Cuthell Calderwood. The judge also accepted the guilty plea by Mary Derrico of manslaughter in the second degree; however, he stated that she was distraught over the death of her friends and that she didn't knowingly give them poisonous alcohol. That, along with her cooperation with U.S. Treasury and local law enforcement, had given him the reasons to forego the maximum sentence of fifteen years. The judge did state that she snuffed out lives with her illegal activities and, as such, had to pay a fine of $500 and be on probation for five years. She was given a suspended sentence of five to ten years at the Bedford Hills, New York Women's State Prison. As long as she lived by the terms of her probation, Mrs. Derrico would not go to prison. The judge did tell her that the terms of her probation included seeing her probation officer weekly, going to her church every week and cutting further association with the liquor-making business.

Justice would not be so light for Salvatore DiBenedetto or his sons, Michael and Phillip. It was discovered by authorities that the men had purchased a large barrel of antifreeze radiator compound from a local service station. It was obvious to authorities that the men had made the liquor but had not intentionally made the beverage poisonous. Salvatore DiBenedetto had been charged with murder in the first degree but pleaded guilty to the lesser charge of manslaughter in the first degree and was sentenced in Oneida County Court to ten to twenty years hard labor in New York State Prison. His sons would be found guilty of lesser charges and sentenced to the Elmira Reformatory.

The mayor of Utica recognized the bravery of Utica lawmen who had surrounded the DiBenedetto home and apprehended the desperate men. Utica police detectives Grieco and Grande, as well as Patrolman Caputo, were given commendations for bravery. The Creeping Death had run its course throughout the Mohawk Valley during that frigid January 1935. Thirty-three people of the valley lost their lives, yet not all of the liquor was seized. Beware, dear reader, for in a wine cellar, perhaps your own, you might just find a bottle of the Creeping Death. Drink at your own risk.

My, How the Sheriff's Garden Grows

Commerce is against morality. Morality is going to lose every time.
—Robin Day

The county jail garden had potatoes, tomatoes and all sorts of perishable vegetables that rewarded the inmates who tended to the garden more gently than the victims of their crimes. Little did anyone know that a vegetable garden in the shadow of the prison walls of a jail overseen by Sheriff Edward Jackson of Fonda would spur one of the most sensationalistic cases of suspected lawman abuse in the history of Montgomery County.

Sheriff Jackson took office on January 3, 1934, and had been considered a stellar man of law enforcement until two years later, when three of the sheriff's employees resigned and wrote an accusatory letter to the governor of New York State that would ignite a firestorm of alleged illegalities and abuses of office. First County Investigator Gervaise Moehringer resigned after serving just twenty-seven months. He'd been appointed by Sheriff Jackson and resigned without giving cause, but it was rumored that he didn't like the way things were being run in the sheriff's department. He would remain silent, but three employees in the department resigned and did write to New York State governor Herbert H. Lehman, listing more than forty specific instances of misuse and abuse of office by Sheriff Edward Jackson. The employees were August H. Ische, William F. Schwartz and William

Rink. Ische and Rink were former jailers, and Schwartz had been the county jail cook and former deputy. Based on the written testimony of the three former employees, Sheriff Jackson was put under investigation.

The twenty-nine pages of charges had nine specific ones considered the most severe: 1) used Montgomery County funds for his own purposes in more than forty instances; 2) converted foodstuffs for his own personal use; 3) neglected and refused to perform his duties as specified by law and his oath of office; 4) refused to accompany deputies when they made serious or emergency calls; 5) didn't properly feed inmates in the county jail; 6) denied basic necessities to inmates in medicine, sheets and towels; 7) refused to let deputies use the office phone in emergencies; 8) created unsafe conditions in the jail by shutting off the lights at an unreasonable hour; and 9) endangering the lives of deputies by sending them out against wrongdoers and not informing them what armaments they would come into contact with. Governor Lehman ordered the district attorney of Montgomery County to perform his constitutional duty and bring the charges to the grand jury. When presented with the charges, Sheriff Jackson called them "childish" and refused to answer them. He denied that he had done anything wrong or committed any kind of malfeasance. He exclaimed that he had nothing to cover up, yet he had no choice. He had to answer the charges as put forth by the governor and the district attorney.

Some of the specific instances included that the sheriff had taken vegetables from the jail garden for his own personal use, and upon serving warrants, summons and executions, he kept the money for himself. Sheriff Jackson hired former Supreme Court justice Newton J. Harrick Sr., as well as Carl Salmon, who prepared a seventy-five-page response to the charges. They asked the governor to dismiss the charges. The case drew large crowds to the courthouse and spurred great drama and rumor among the citizenry. During the grand jury inquiry, the district attorney called sixty-nine witnesses and showed more than two hundred exhibits. The trial lasted from October 12 to October 26 without a break from sundown to sunset. In response to this, the sheriff's attorneys presented a signed affidavit by prisoners that stated that the food served was adequate. Also, Dr. J. Howard Crosby of Fultonville, who was the prison doctor, signed an affidavit that he inspected the inmates and declared that they did not appear to be in any adverse condition.

Sheriff Jackson admitted that his recordkeeping was sloppy and that he only took items from the garden if there was an abundance and the items were going to spoil. The grand jury ended up not charging the sheriff with any wrongdoing. It could not be proven that the sheriff had kept any money, and it was discovered that one of the men who had resigned and testified had also taken potatoes from the jail's garden. What the grand jury did do was sign off on twenty resolutions, including ordering Sheriff Jackson to keep a cash book and create a docket for all cash transactions; a resolution was also created commending the district attorney for how he conducted the investigation. All in all, it was a lot of ballyhoo, time and expense on how the sheriff grew his garden.

The Chicken Roost Gang

I know my hens like I know my wife and children.
—farmer victimized by the Chicken Roost Gang

Farmers throughout Otsego and Schoharie Counties had been reporting to the sheriff of bandits coming onto their farmlands at night and stealing entire flocks of chickens. The best minds in the law departments of both counties were put on the case, coming up with a moniker for the perpetrators—the "Chicken Roost Gang"—for they surmised that the crimes couldn't have been committed by a single individual. The quickness of the roundup and the cart-off had to have been accomplished by a group, and an experienced group at that, perhaps even neighboring farmers.

All over both counties, farmers sat in coops with shotguns at their chests, waiting for the dastardly Chicken Roost Gang to come and attempt to commandeer their chicks. With the price of chickens up to an all-time high (ten cents per pound), the incentive was there for thieves to make good money, yet it was surmised that members of the Chicken Roost Gang were using gas-powered vehicles to make the long treks out to the rural farms across two counties. This was considered an expensive venture by law enforcement considering that gasoline had risen to the almost unheard-of price of ten cents per gallon. Police knew that the Chicken Roost Gang had to steal an ample amount of chickens in order to cover the mileage expense.

The Chicken Roost Gang terrorized fowl on many farms. *Art by Dennis Webster.*

The members of the Chicken Roost Gang were finally apprehended by lawmen after being spotted by an eagle-eyed farmer as they fled the scene of their latest theft. They were caught with the chickens in their possession, later identified out of a lineup by a savvy farmer who made it his business to know each one of his chickens personally. "I know my hens like I know my wife and children," stated the farmer.

The shocking discovery by law enforcement in the two victimized and terrorized counties was that the Chicken Roost Gang had been a family affair. Arrested and charged with the theft and insidious movement of poultry across county lines in Otsego and Schoharie were the father, Marvin Banks; the mother, Anna Banks; and their two sons, Charles Banks and Chancy Banks—all of Sharon Springs. The chicken-stealing brood was brought in front of Judge Harold D. Carpenter and held on the charge of third-degree burglary. They were held in the Schoharie County Jail until they were brought to trial and found guilty of chicken theft. They were then transferred to Otsego County, charged, tried and found guilty of the same theft of countywide chickens. Farmers and their poultry were much appeased at the apprehension, trial and conviction of the Chicken Roost Gang. Some farmers, however, preferred to stay sleeping in their coops after discovering the enjoyment that one could have with the content clucking clan.

His Numbers Didn't Add Up

I'm gettin' going, fellas. You're playin' a dirty trick on me.
—last earthly words of Edward Reali before he was murdered

SCHENECTADY, NEW YORK, 1944

Edward Reali, thirty-six, usually sold newspapers, but tough times forced him to take on the selling of "numbers" as a way to supplement his income. The system operated when people picked a number of the day, got a ticket with that number and paid a rate to the bookie, who took in all the money and forwarded that cash to an upper-echelon boss. If you picked the correct number, you'd win cash, but that was a low payout in comparison to the assets collected by crime bosses. Numbers running was usually given to organized crime rookies or low-level men. These "numbers" rackets were illegal and made organized crime factions a lot of money until the states declared the lotteries legal. Running numbers usually took place at corner stores, grocery stores, bars and diners. The racket has always been one of the ways organized crime has profited without much of an effort, yet even up to his death, Mr. Reali never revealed his connections to where he funneled the money, to the point where even his wife under testimony in court didn't know her husband's numbers-running cohorts or who his boss was—only that he was "employee #309." Edward Reali would pay for this illegal activity with his life, as he was murdered and dumped in the Mohawk River by two young men seeking to rob the numbers runner of his wad of cash.

Frank Rossi Jr., or "Junior," as he was called, and Damon W. Stendor, both nineteen years old, committed the murder and confessed to the crime. As details of their deed and the ensuing trial hit the public, the sleepy town was shocked at the audacity and the gore of the crime. The full details came out in the confessions that Rossi and Stendor gave to police authorities. Stendor ended up signing his confession, while Rossi dictated it to the New York State Police and then backed off on signing it, although the *Schenectady Gazette* printed the entire confessions of both boys.

Rossi had stated that he had been employed as a contractor working for his father and had previously been discharged from the army. In his confession, Rossi ran through the entire events of the evening. It was a hot and muggy Mohawk Valley night on August 8, 1944, when Rossi picked up Stendor, whom he had only known for four months, and stopped in front of Rudolph's Jewelry Store on the corner of Broadway and State Street in order to pick a number from Edward Reali. Rossi chose number 532 and paid Reali twenty-five cents. Rossi had known the numbers man for three years and had always observed the man picking up his newspapers at midnight and then delivering them while selling numbers to the night owls all over the city. Rossi, after selecting and paying for his numbers, drove with Stendor to a Greek diner, where the insidious crime was hatched.

ROSSI'S CONFESSION

The following is part of the text of Rossi's confession:

> *Stendor told me that Reali carried a lot of cash and had also said, "Let's grab him and kill him." [My] response was "But that's murder. Why do that?" We talked for a little while then I agreed with Stendor and told him, "Alright, lets do it." We drove around until 5:45 a.m. when we saw him standing outside the Modern Diner. We offered to drive him around to his stops so he picked up his large pile of newspapers and got into the front seat with Damon Stendor getting in the back. We stopped at White Tower where Reali delivered some newspapers and sold some numbers. When we were alone in the car, I told Damon that we would drive to Aqueduct and take him out there and rob his money. I told him to wait for my whistle then hit Reali from behind. I drove out to the place that was off the beaten path just outside the city and onto a dirt road. We*

got out and I whistled yet Damon didn't make a move so we got back in the car and drove deeper into the woods until we were right by the banks of the Mohawk River. I stopped the car and got out with a screwdriver, popped the hood and pretended that I had car trouble. It was at this point that Reali got out of the car with his stack of newspapers under his arm and said, "I'm gettin' going, fellas. You're playin' a dirty trick on me." I waited until he was away from the car and I ran him down from behind and knocked him to the ground where we were scuffling. Damon came out of the car with a hammer and cracked Reali in the back of the head so hard, the handle snapped off. Reali fell to the ground and I told Damon to go back to the car and get the engine crank. As he did I kicked Reali in the face and stomped on his neck. Damon came back and cracked Reali in the back of the head one last time. We rifled through his pockets and took all his money. We both dragged the body about fifty feet to the banks of the Mohawk River and tossed him down but he was only partially in the water so I went down and dragged him into the deeper part of the river. He was floating and I kept pushing his body down until he finally sank. Damon went and picked up the bloody newspapers and threw them in my car. We drove down a ways then piled them up on the ground and set fire to them to get rid of the evidence. We then drove to Damon's house where he took off his bloody shirt and stuffed it behind his dresser while I took off my wet clothes and put on a pair of his trousers and a shirt. We counted out the money and we had $247 and we both split the cash. We went and got something to eat then I dropped off Damon and that's the last I talked with him.

This confession by Rossi would be almost identical to the one dictated and signed by Damon Stendor, except that Stendor claimed that Rossi was the one with the original idea to kill Reali. It would be a few days before Virgil Sauter, while canoeing, found Reali's bloated dead body floating in the Mohawk River about five hundred feet from where the murder had occurred. Witnesses had seen the teens driving Reali around the city and went to police with their stories. The boys were picked up, and they confessed after twelve hours of interrogation, although later in the trial, the defense would say that the boys had been beaten by police until they confessed. Police Chief John J. McGovern found the bloody shirt at Stendor's house behind the dresser, right where he told the chief it would be. The police also took the lads to the scene of the crime and found the hammer handle there. Rossi later claimed that the police had teased him that he could get away if he could swim the Mohawk River in handcuffs. The claims of physical and verbal abuse were steadfastly denied by the police officers involved.

The boys were both charged with first-degree murder and would be tried together. They both pleaded not guilty. Justice Andrew Ryan was the presiding judge, with District Attorney William M. Nicoll as the prosecuting attorney; the defense was handled by lawyers James Leary and Jacob Frankel. The trial would be swift, as the jury was selected rather quickly, and the evidence of the boys' confession, along with the recovered evidence, would prove to be a difficult case for the defense. The testimony of Dr. E.J. Senn, coroner, stunned the audience with a description of the state

Damon Stendor's mug shot. *Old Fulton New York Post Cards, fultonhistory.com.*

of Reali's body—this in front of the murdered man's wife, who dabbed tears and sobbed at the details. Reali's sister found her brother's face so badly disfigured that she could only identify him by a scar on his shoulder, an appendix scar and his clothes.

Dr. Senn described Reali's body as being black in color, with a swollen face and eyes bulging right out of his skull. The doctor declared the death as being a result of a severely compound fractured skull, including lacerations to the brain and brain hemorrhage. Reali also had a broken nose and bruises on his neck. The body was so swollen from the river that the skin was splitting and peeling away. Ladies in the courtroom gasped, and those with weak constitutions left the courtroom holding their stomachs from the grisly details. The injuries were consistent with the confessions given by the boys.

During the trial, as witnesses testified, it was reported that Stendor was nervous, his eyes darting back and forth, while Rossi stared them down with eyes as black as gun bores, without a fleck of emotion, wearing a crucifix around his neck, which he held in his hand and constantly thumbed. The good looks of the lads did not go unnoticed by several female fans, dubbed the "Bobby Sox" by the media. These young women were at every session, watching the good-looking boys with a doe-eyed fascination that many couldn't understand or explain. The main witness was Trooper James Finn, whom Rossi had claimed beat him into a confession. Finn denied the accusation. He had sat in the back seat of the police car with Rossi as two officers sat in the front. These other officers heard the entire conversation in which Rossi claimed that he had heard that Reali was dead and had drowned in the Mohawk River. After a while, Rossi admitted that he'd killed Reali.

The big dramatic turn was when Stendor asked to take the stand because he had something to say. His attorney suggested that he not do this, yet he couldn't be swayed. Once on the stand, Stendor claimed that Rossi wasn't with him and that he alone had committed the crime, although this was in direct contrast to the confession that he had dictated and signed. His testimony would be a blip on the radar screen, as the police officers' testimony and the signed confessions would stand as more solid evidence than Stendor's new testimony.

The members of the defense had their work cut out for them, as they couldn't prove the coerced confessions. They attempted to question the coroner on whether the injuries to Reali could have happened after he drowned in the river. "Yes," declared the coroner. This was all the defense had before the jury retired to deliberate. Within hours, they came back and found the boys guilty of the crime as charged. The defense then attempted to restrict the lads' sentences to twenty years as they pleaded for leniency from the judge. Damon Stendor had been raised in an orphanage after his abandonment by his mentally ill mother and abusive father. He had been deemed psychotic and was discharged by the army for this, as well as being feebleminded. Rossi was stated to have had epilepsy and was deemed to be of "borderline intelligence," which meant that he had the approximate mental ability of a ten-year-old. Judge Ryan ignored these pleas and gave the teens on December 21, 1944,

Justice Andrew W. Ryan. *Old Fulton New York Post Cards, fultonhistory.com.*

the maximum sentence of thirty-five years to life, to be served at Clinton Prison in Dannemora, New York.

On their way out of court, reporters yelled out to the lads for a statement, with Rossi saying, "I wasn't given a fair trial," while Stendor would only mutter under his breath, "I haven't anything to say." One bizarre incident regarding the Bobby Sox girls stunned Stendor. One came forward and gave his defense attorney a Christmas present for Damon, which he later opened in jail to find a brand-new bow tie that was highly in fashion at the time. Stendor laughed at the gift and gave the present to one of the jail employees. It was said that Stendor was mesmerized by the underworld. Reali was a simple newspaper deliveryman attempting to make extra cash for his family. Even though running numbers was against the law, the man paid for it with his life. For one fateful evening, employee no. 309's numbers didn't add up.

What's On the Menu at Uncle Henry's Pancake House?

You have been convicted of conducting a loathsome, degrading and illegal business
and you must pay the penalty.
—Judge Hanagan upon sentencing Henry Cittadino
to running a house of ill repute

UTICA, NEW YORK, 1944

Henry Cittadino was just thirty-two years old when he was convicted in 1944 of operating a brothel, or "disorderly house," as it was called by Judge Hanagan, who presided over the case. This would be the beginning of a long life of such operation charges for Mr. Cittadino, and wife, Beatrice, who would be charged right along with him, but this time it was not out of the infamous Uncle Henry's Pancake House on LaFayette Street in Utica. Instead, it was for operating a brothel in a slum house at 232 Water Street, a home that was torn down soon after.

In this case, Henry Cittadino was given six months in jail. Maurice Supiro was his attorney and asked for leniency in the trial by stating that the testimony used to convict his client was "contradictory and conflicting" and that it was given by a "self-confessed prostitute who came to Utica and created an upheaval the like of which has not been known here in twenty five years or more." He also asked the judge to think of the testimony and that the property had been condemned and would soon be torn down for the Second Ward Housing Project. Supirc also stated that the testimony given had been tainted by a jailhouse conspiracy between the prostitute and a married man she used to help her case. Judge Hanagan was not moved by the attorney and declared that although the testimony wasn't perfect, it was sufficient from a legal standpoint.

"Cittadino," said the judge, "you have been convicted of conducting a loathsome, degrading and illegal business and you must pay the penalty." Upon his sentence, Cittadino confessed to three previous convictions, including third-degree assault. In 1927, he served eighteen months in Randall's Island for delinquency and procurement and had been arrested twelve times for law violations, including petit larceny, third-degree assault and violation of probation. Henry did not learn his lesson from this prison stint and went on to create a place at which the menu served hot buttery flapjacks and, upstairs, a breakfast of the flesh. In the legend of the place, it's always called Uncle Henry's Pancake House, yet all of the ads from the time and the sign on the front of the establishment referred to it as Uncle Henry's Pancake Restaurant.

Newspaper ad from Uncle Henry's Pancake Restaurant. *Old Fulton New York Post Cards, fultonhistory.com.*

In 1953, District Attorney John M. Liddy padlocked the Cittadino property, as he and his wife were under investigation for running a brothel; however, it wasn't until March 1958 that Henry and Beatrice Cittadino would make front-page news in the Mohawk Valley with their arrest in Miami. The Oneida County Grand Jury had decided to investigate and fight vice in the county and the city of Utica. District Attorney Liddy sent two Oneida County sheriff's deputies, Thomas Abounader and Robert Ingalls, to Dade County, Florida, to make the arrests based on a sealed indictment against the Cittadinos that charged them with keeping a disorderly house and disorderly conduct.

The arrest in Florida continued the string of arrests for prostitution for the Cittadinos. January 1959 would see Henry and Beatrice arrested for felony prostitution and for running a brothel out of their restaurant. The charges would be nine felony counts and four misdemeanor counts. Henry and Beatrice were still out on bail from their 1958 arrest when the newest charges were filed, superseding the previous charges. March 1959 would see Henry pleading guilty to reduced charges on the eve of his and his wife's trial, thus getting one year in jail while Beatrice got a one-year suspended sentence. This caused Henry and Beatrice to see the error of their ways, and they stayed out of trouble with the law. However, bad karma struck Henry on June 1969 when he was assaulted in his restaurant by an enraged customer. David Sgroi, twenty-seven, went ballistic and hit Henry over the head with a chair from the restaurant, smashed dishes and spewed colorful metaphors that are still hanging over the Mohawk Valley. Sgroi was arrested and charged with assault, disorderly conduct, criminal mischief and abusive language and was sentenced by Justice Eugene Sullivan to one year in Oneida County Jail and fined $150.

Uncle Henry's Pancake Restaurant. *Oneida County Historical Society.*

In the 1970s, Uncle Henry's Pancake House was transformed from a flapjack eatery that also hosted payment for flesh services to a sunny-side-up and buttered-toast power center for Utica Democrats after Marino's Restaurant (also known as "Little City Hall") was torn down. In the twenty-first century, Uncle Henry's Pancake House evokes fond memories for many in the Mohawk Valley as the place where one could get hot food, discuss politics and be served special desserts. Today the establishment is thought of quite fondly as a place and operation long gone, a part of a different time and age when such operations were not unusual in any city in the United States. It was one of at least five brothels that were operating in Utica at the time, but memories of it are the most well known.

My Mommy the Axe Murderer

Burton can't live long, come right away.
—Bessie Grabo on the phone to her sister
right after killing her own son with an axe

ROTTERDAM, NEW YORK, 1947

Nothing says "I love you" like twenty axe chops to the face. For Bessie Grabo, who was sixty-three years old, she believed that hacking her son's skull to a mushy pulp was the only way to keep her family together. It was allegedly out of love and devotion to her child that she committed the most insidious crime a mother can commit: the murder of her own offspring. Bessie Grabo had struggled her entire life with a debilitating mental illness, and on a sweltering August night in the Mohawk Valley, her fear, paranoia and love culminated in her loving axe swings. Her beloved son, Burton Grabo, a broom salesman forty-one years old, had been committed to the Utica State Hospital for the Insane three years earlier, and she feared that he was going to be forced to go back. Her husband, George Grabo, an insurance salesman by trade, had left her in what was soon to be a divorce, and now she feared that her son would be recommitted. She couldn't be alone. The axe would unite them in the afterlife. Forever.

Eight years earlier, in 1939, Bessie Grabo had been committed to a health facility for treatment of her mental illness and for attempting suicide by cutting her throat with a razor blade. Her son had followed in her mental health footsteps when he was admitted and treated for his ailment at the Utica State Hospital for the Insane, where the Utica crib had been invented, which was a cage that was bolted down to the patient's bed. It was early in the morning when Ida Giddings, Bessie's sister who lived in Gloversville, received a phone call from her sibling with the cryptic message, "Burton can't live long, come right away." Bessie then hung up. Ida rushed over to her sister's home and made the grisly discovery of her nephew's dead body on the couch. His face had been hacked to a pulp, so identification wasn't instantaneous, but she recognized her nephew's clothing and body type, so she knew that her sister had murdered Burton. Ida called the police, who found the bloody axe in the basement, yet there was no Bessie in or about the home. The Schenectady County coroner, E.J. Sehn, was called to the scene and, after a quick examination, declared that "[i]t seems like a pretty clear case of murder." He suggested the time of death to be 5:30 a.m. and that the man had been the victim of more than twenty blows from an axe. Bessie had hacked her son's head so much that she had chopped down to Burton's neck and throat. The authorities paused to look at the framed replication of the famous painting *Whistler's Mother* that hung a few feet above where the man lay dead on the blood-splattered couch.

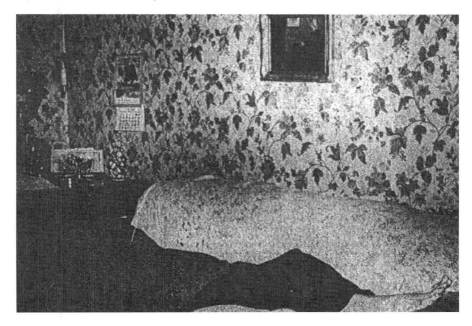

The corpse of Burton Grabo on his mother's couch, where he was murdered in his sleep. Note the painting *Whistler's Mother* on the wall above Grabo's body. *Old Fulton New York Post Cards, fultonhistory.com.*

The authorities were put on high alert seeking Bessie Grabo. Where was she? Bessie was soon pulled from the chilling waters of the Mohawk River ten miles down the road. Two lads, Leo Strong and John Quinlan, had heard Bessie's cry for help and found the woman sitting in the middle of the Mohawk River, the flowing water up to her chin. The boys helped her out and discovered that she had a slit throat, and she kept repeating over and over in a deadpan monotone, "I've killed my son. I've killed my son." The Scotia Fire Department Ambulance was dispatched and brought her to Ellis Hospital, where later she did not deny the murder yet showed no remorse as police arrested her at the hospital under the charge of first-degree murder. Assistant District Attorney Emmett Lynch had her sign a statement in which she admitted to hacking her son to death. Her story stunned the police authorities, who listened intently as the woman spoke in a calm manner of her deed.

Bessie spoke even though her neck had been bandaged from the self-inflicted wound. She was matter-of-fact as she spoke:

> *I had asked my son to come over to my home. I went to bed at eleven at night and he wasn't over yet. I woke up at five-thirty in the morning and came downstairs to see my beloved Burton asleep on my couch. I stared lovingly at his peacefulness and whispered, "You poor, sweet boy, you look so nice but have no home and in four weeks will be alone." I then went over to the window and stared outside for a few moments pondering my life and it's at this point I had the epiphany that I would end his life and mine. I went to the cellar and retrieved the axe. I swung with all my might and struck him in the face. His head jerked yet he never woke up or made a sound. When I was finished I put the axe back downstairs. I went upstairs to my room to change out of my night clothes and into my outdoor clothes. I came down to my kitchen and took out my butcher knife. I ran my thumb across the blade and it was dull so I took my time sharpening it before I put it in my purse. I called Ida then walked to the bus stop. I took the bus a while down the road then departed and walked a little bit before I came to the river. I took out the butcher knife and dragged it across my throat. I dropped it and my purse on the bank of the Mohawk. I wandered out into the river to drown myself but I soon discovered that it was too shallow. No matter how many times I dove under, I kept coming back up. It was then that I tried to drown by gulping the river water. I just couldn't kill myself so I sat down in the river and called out for help. Those nice young men saved me.*

Police were stunned at her emotionless tone. She said that she loved her son more than anything in this world and did it so they could be together. The police stood guard at her bedside until she could be examined by two court-appointed psychiatrists who had been called in by District Attorney William Nicoll. The psychiatrists were Dr. J.M. Scott and Dr. Walter Clark of Schenectady, who both agreed that Bessie Grabo was indeed mentally ill and had her committed to Matteawan State Hospital for the Insane. Judge James W. Liddle signed the order and declared that Bessie would be arraigned for first-degree murder but not until she was declared free of her mental health afflictions and not until "she is restored to her right mind." Bessie continued to declare that she was not responsible for her actions and that she had been afraid that her son was going to be put back in the mental hospital. It was reported that Bessie was at peace in her room at Matteawan State Hospital for the Insane, declaring, "I love my son."

The Political Power Broker of Utica

I'm no angel, but I'm not the devil either.
—Rufus P. "Rufie" Elefante

Utica, New York

The world of politics was in a golden age in the United States during the decades from the 1930s to the 1950s, and no politically influential person wielded more power in his beloved city than Rufus "Rufie" Elefante in Utica during this glorious time, dispensing jobs and political favors from his booth at his beloved Marino's Restaurant. He was raised by Italian immigrant parents in a city that had undergone drastic cultural change. Rufus had been attracted to politics at a very young age and immersed himself first with the Republican Party but then switched and stuck with the Democrats for most of his career and life. It would be his solid democratic east Utica political bloc that would take Utica to new heights.

As a young man, Rufus aligned himself with the powerful west Utica Irish political boss Charles Donnelly. When the stock market crashed and the Great Depression hit the entire country, Rufus rallied the hardworking yet underpaid immigrants to go against the wealthy textile mill owners for improved wages and conditions. Rufus was very young but had a solid group of supporters, as well as the Italian voters of east Utica, in solidarity for the Democratic Party. He used his polity savvy to build the strength and reputation of this bloc to assist Franklin D. Roosevelt in his 1928 victory as the New York governor when he delivered ten thousand voters to a rally in Utica that garnered statewide attention. He also delivered key votes to the victory of New York State governor Alfred E. Smith. These moves would pay dividends to Utica in New Deal projects that would provide much-needed jobs for Utica citizens, all thanks to the political power of Rufus Elefante, a man who never had nor ever would hold an elected office.

It was this old-fashioned "honest graft," as it was referred to, that solidified his power. Rufus handed out jobs from his booth at Marino's Restaurant to flocks of Uticans eager to make a better living for their

Rufus "Rufie" Elefante. *Oneida County Historical Society.*

families. His own trucking company also improved because of all the jobs and industry he was bringing to Utica. Many said that this was an evil or illegal practice, yet the man was never charged with nor convicted of a crime. The world of politics can be a dirty and nasty business, yet Rufie worked for the city and the people he loved as much as he did for his private service.

New York governor Thomas Dewey, though, was so incensed at not carrying Oneida County in his failed presidential bid that he came after Rufie. Many felt that the powerful bloc of voters that Rufie delivered to Truman had kept Dewey from winning the county. As the New York governor, Dewey tried to prosecute Rufus on a violation of election laws in 1943 by stating that he had paid voters. Rufus Elefante was quickly and easily acquitted of all charges.

Rufie Elefante was described as a handsome, well-dressed man who had a quick wit and a wonderful sense of humor. He was a man beloved by many, yet some stated that he had too strong a stranglehold on the selections to political office in Utica. However, the voters in the city kept electing his choices, demonstrating that the citizenry was happy overall with what Rufie was offering. Many people in Utica achieved a better life economically because of his influence, yet some felt frustration in facing off against Rufie and his selected politicians. Many, including the *Observer-Dispatch* newspaper, referred to Rufie's hangout, Marino's Restaurant, as "Little City Hall." His power base would stay at the popular eatery until 1972, when it was torn down for urban renewal. Rufie then held meetings at Uncle Henry's Pancake House.

It wasn't until the 1970s that Rufie would drift from his beloved Democratic Party when he supported Ed Hanna, independent candidate for Utica mayor. Hanna appointed Rufus as a "special advisor" and declared April 7, 1974, to be "Rufus P. Elefante Day." This relationship lasted six months before Rufus went back to the Democratic Party and supported (and got elected) Stephen Pawlinga in 1977. It was more than handing out patronage in a booth at a restaurant that would cement Elefante's reputation; it was his savvy moves inside and outside the party that, even into the late 1970s and 1980s, garnered respect and frustration from opponents of his choosing.

The *Observer Dispatch* editor, William Lohden, had superimposed Utica City Hall Tower on top of Marino's Restaurant to illustrate where Utica political power was meted out. *Oneida County Historical Society.*

Political cartoon on Elefante's political power. *Oneida County Historical Society.*

In 1981, Utica Republican mayoral candidate Robert Cardillo stated about Rufie that "political bosses are a dying breed and he's one of the best. He runs that Democratic organization with a tight fist." Louis LaPolla at this time called Rufus "a veteran politician with a great deal of influence." Although most scholars would say that Rufus Elefante's real power only lasted from the years 1928 to 1958, the truth is that the man garnered respect and influence until his passing at the age of ninety-one in 1994.

Political power brokers like Rufus Elefante will never exist again in this country, and his maneuvering assisted many in Utica in expanding and improving their economic statures. When textile mills started to leave Utica, it was Rufus Elefante who used his political strength and connections to bring Griffiss Air Force Base to Rome, New York, along with Utica businesses Chicago Pneumatic, Bendix and General Electric among others. These businesses provided upward mobility and high-paying manufacturing jobs that helped Utica swell to great heights. This was amazing for a man who had never held elected office yet wielded what some would say was the greatest power in the history of the city of Utica. Even today, many years after his passing, Uticans marvel at the man and what he achieved. Some long for the days when you could get a job just by visiting Rufie at his booth at Marino's. It was Rufus Elefante himself who best described his political and personal personality: "I'm no angel, but I'm not the devil either."

Mr. Big

Kingpin of the Upstate rackets.
—Myles J. Lane, chairman of the Legislative Watchdog Committee,
referring to the role of Joseph Falcone

UTICA, NEW YORK

Joseph Falcone and his older brother, Salvatore, immigrated to New York City from Sicily in the early twentieth century, eventually moving to Utica, New York, as young men looking to fulfill their American dream. Joseph and his brother ran their own businesses; the onset of prohibition changed everything for the brothers. Joseph and Salvatore built their business by selling sugar, yeast and other supplies that would eventually lead to them being charged with alcohol conspiracy in 1940 for supplying items that law enforcement said could assist illegal still operators. They were convicted, but their case was thrown out by the United States Supreme Court, as it was determined that selling these kinds of supplies didn't prove conspiracy. This cleaned the records of the Falcones, and neither Joseph nor Salvatore was ever charged with a crime or convicted of anything for the rest of their lives.

For the rest of his life, Joseph Falcone was named by law enforcement, the media and politicians as "Mr. Big." In Utica, he was talked about as the man who ran what was referred to in those days as "the mob." This was something that was never explicitly proven. Utica was no different than any other small, thriving city in the mid-twentieth century, with gambling,

Left: Joseph Falcone. *Oneida County Historical Society.*

Below: Salvatore Falcone's grocery store. *Oneida County Historical Society.*

prostitution and other vices, but it was always thought that Joseph Falcone was the man running the show. His older brother Salvatore moved to Miami in the 1940s to run a grocery store. Authorities attempted to deport the Falcone brothers but were unsuccessful.

APALACHIN MEETING

On November 14, 1957, an event happened that exposed the mob (or Cosa Nostra) to the United States and especially to Federal Bureau of Investigation (FBI) director J. Edgar Hoover, who had been in denial that such an organization existed. Joseph Falcone and Salvatore Falcone were in attendance at an American mafia meeting held in Apalachin, New York, where about one hundred of the most powerful mobsters in the United States gathered. They met at the fifty-two-acre rural home of Joseph "the Barber" Barbara, a place that had only one road leading up to the house and had fields and woods surrounding it.

The strange license plates on expensive automobiles and numerous bookings to local motels caught the attention of state police sergeant Edgar D. Croswell, who had held a personal vendetta against Barbara for some time. He had attempted to prove that Barbara was a gangster, and with the massive criminal enclave, he had his chance. A contingency of law enforcement—including Sergeant Croswell, his partner, two agents from the U.S. Treasury and fifteen New York state troopers—drove up the driveway to the Barbara house on McFall Road, blocking escape. As the lawmen pulled up to the house, they caught the group eating barbecue. Law enforcement described what happened next as something out of an Abbott and Costello movie. Men dropped their plates and scattered, running in all directions into the woods, with many getting easily caught. The mobsters were wearing expensive watches, jewelry, fine suits and hats and trench coats, all of which made an escape into the woods difficult, with many getting snagged on branches and leaping through fields in their patent leather wingtips that would get sucked into the muddy bog.

The law enforcement contingency retreated and placed a roadblock at the only road out of Barbara's house. More than sixty underworld bosses were detained and arraigned. Ultimately, nobody was convicted with anything to do with the meeting, but for the members of the Cosa Nostra, it was a major embarrassment and exposure for those who chose to remain behind the scenes. Twenty-two of the attendees were arrested and charged with conspiracy and contempt by the Justice Department of the United States, yet all of the charges were thrown out as unconstitutional in 1960 by the U.S. Court of Appeals. The exact reasons for the meeting were never discovered, but it did force J. Edgar Hoover to admit to the existence of the mob in America and to then form his "Top Hoodlum Program."

Joseph Falcone and his older brother, Salvatore, were never charged with anything at all connected with the Apalachin meeting, but it did bring unwanted attention to many of the men in attendance. As a result of this exposure, Joseph Falcone had his real estate, liquor and notary public licenses revoked by the New York State Division of Licenses. This was handed down by the secretary of the division, who publicly stated that the meeting was no accident and that "Falcone's conduct was disorderly and he consorted with persons of evil reputation and who partook in infamous crimes and offenses which amounted to moral turpitude and is grounds for revocation." In 1959, Robert Kennedy, at the time counsel for the New York Senate Rackets Committee, said that Falcone was "one of ten men in the country involved in the coin machine business." What was amazing was that Joseph Falcone had his licenses stripped and had these public statements made about him, yet he never had been convicted of any crime whatsoever. Not having the liquor license would have been harmful since Joseph Falcone ran the Utica Retail Liquor Company on Bleecker Street in Utica, New York.

LEGISLATIVE WATCHDOG COMMITTEE

In 1958, the New York State Legislative Watchdog Committee was put together to look into vice activities in New York State, including Utica. The committee was composed of four New York State senators and four New York State assemblymen, along with the chairman, Myles J. Lane, who called Joseph Falcone the "kingpin of the Upstate rackets." The watchdog committee subpoenaed Joseph Falcone, and he did not show due to health reasons on the set date, so a warrant was issued, and he eventually agreed to testify on February 1958 at 42 West Forty-fourth Street in New York City. Before Joseph took the stand, the most dramatic part of the testimony had come from New York State police sergeant Ray Fogerty, who worked out of Troop D in Oneida, New York. Sergeant Fogerty testified that he thought

Joseph Falcone was "Mr. Big" in Utica racketeering, yet he admitted under oath that he had no proof.

Sergeant Fogerty also admitted that he had told *Journal American* reporter Dom Frasca that Joseph Falcone and his brother Salvatore ran Utica's gambling rackets and had been responsible for at least thirteen murders over the past twenty-five years, including the unsolved murder of Frank Caputo in 1954. Caputo had supposedly robbed a card game run by the Falcones and was later found dead in the trunk of his car behind an elementary school in Frankfort, New York. Again, Sergeant Fogerty had no proof that Joseph and Salvatore Falcone had anything to do with the unsolved murders. When the watchdog committee's counsel, Arnold Bauman, finally put Joseph Falcone on the stand, he only got answers to what his name was and where he lived. For the rest of the questions, Joseph invoked the Fifth Amendment, eighty-four times, refusing to answer forty-two questions and invoking his constitutional privilege to not incriminate himself thirty-two times.

UNSOLVED MURDERS

When Sergeant Fogerty referred to unsolved murders in Utica, he was specifically referencing ones from the 1920s to the 1950s. This included, in the 1920s, Fred D'Augustino, Louis Spefadora, Eli Yonko, Ciro Gargano and Rosario Gambino. In the 1930s, it included Louis and Rocco Malkoon, Paul Basile, Phillip DiSalvo, Fred LaTella, Dominick Aiello and Pietro Lima. In the 1940s, it included Fred Morelli. In the 1950s, it included Frank Caputo, Paul Carlesimo and Mariano "Happy" Longo. All of these men were shot, strangled, thrown in the barge canal, stuffed into trunks of cars or simply never seen or heard from again. None of these murders was ever solved, and Joseph Falcone was never accused, charged or tried for any of these murders. In the book *The Way of the Wiseguy* by Joseph D. Pistone, he states quite clearly that people hit by the mob tend to be people somehow involved in the business and very rarely anybody else. Pistone also noted that "[w]iseguys do not go around killing people for no good reason. Like I said, if you read in the paper about some guy getting wacked, it's a really good bet he was either a made guy who somehow messed up, or some poor guy who got in over his head with wiseguys and paid the ultimate price."

CRIMINALITY, PUBLICITY AND THE AFTERMATH

All of the attention from Apalachin and the New York State Watchdog Committee brought a lot of negative publicity to the city of Utica, with a scathing article by the *Journal American* using the phrase "Sin City of the East." This was followed by a February 24, 1958 article in *Newsweek* that noted that "Utica is the town gangsters own. It is a wide open town where the brothels and the call girls operate under the tolerant eye of the cops. It is the headquarters town for big time mafia operations in most of the eastern United States that reaches all the way to Cuba." On top of this, the *Observer-Dispatch* and the *Daily Press* had begun their own reporting of political favoritism and corruption in the city—state-appointed prosecutor Robert Fischer had taken over for an ineffectual district attorney John Liddy and Utica's deputy police chief, Vincent Fiore, had resigned, among other shakeups in government. The resulting articles caused the reporters from both newspapers to receive death threats, but ultimately both newspapers persevered and were rewarded with the Pulitzer Prize for their reporting. Unfortunately, for a proud city like Utica, the country-wide public relations damage had been done. There was now no difference between Utica, New York, in the 1950s (regarding vice and crime) and places like Columbus, Ohio, and St. Louis, Missouri. At the time, Utica was at its height in population, with more than 100,000 residents, plenty of high-paying manufacturing jobs and a thriving downtown.

So what is the legacy of Joseph Falcone? For many, it was a man committed to his family and friends, a gentleman with salt-and-pepper hair, dapper clothes and a regal manner. The romanticism of the era makes many remember the time and the man fondly. Joseph Falcone is a man regarded with admiration and awe by those who remember him. He was a man who loved his city. Joseph Falcone passed away on March 27, 1992, at the age of ninety. It was the end of a colorful man and a tie to the glorious past.

Dragged Behind a Car
on Potato Hill Road

Sympathy, prejudice, and bias are human emotions but they have no place in the courtroom or the jury room.
—Judge Walsh to the jury at the Bernard Phillip Hatch trial

STEUFEN, NEW YORK, 1973

The farmer was driving his tractor along Potato Hill Road on April 26, 1973, hauling a load of brush, when he spotted a green car dragging something white behind it. James Weaver was witnessing the gruesome dragging death of Mary Rose Turner. At the time, the farmer didn't think that it was anything nefarious. "It was a wonder I stopped after seeing the car dragging an item. I thought someone was married and was dragging something behind the bridal car," said Weaver. "I stopped to investigate when I saw blood and other things along the road." James Weaver had become the prime witness to a murder and subsequent trial that would come to be the lengthiest and costliest in the history of Oneida County.

THE CRIME

Mary Rose Turner, fifty-six, worked as a stenographer for the Oneida County Welfare Department and was missing at the time of the incident. When James Weaver reported what he saw to the police, the drag marks of

The shallow grave of Mary Rose Turner was discovered on Latteiman Road. *Photo by Ashley Webster.*

what the investigators surmised was perhaps a human body were nine miles in length down Potato Hill Road. Investigators set up roadblocks and asked for witnesses to come forward if they had spotted a green car in the area. In the meantime, multiple witnesses told authorities of having seen Bernard Phillip Hatch driving his green car in the area of Latteiman Road, Steuben, at the time of the dragging. Police investigators came upon what looked like a freshly dug grave site right off Latteiman Road, right next to Potato Hill Road. On a bitter spring day that had a mixture of rain and snow, the police authorities discovered a woman's body with the hands and feet cut off in only one foot of soil.

The woman also had no teeth, as they had been removed, and the most shocking discovery of all was that the face of the woman had been sliced off. The only reason a killer would do this would be to try to hide the identity of the victim. To hardened and upstanding law officers, seeing the malicious mutilation of a vulnerable human being was shocking. The murder also stunned the small town of Steuben, a heavenly slice of lush trees and rolling farmlands toiled by honest and hardworking people. On April 28, troopers set up a command post and roadblock to question other possible witnesses. Sergeant Romaine B. Gallo was manning the roadblock and was standing near a New York State police helicopter when a man sped by in a green 1966 two-door car. There was a female passenger, and the male driver had long hair, a lengthy mustache and sideburns. The car kept going, so Sergeant Gallo gave chase and ran fifty feet to the road, picking up "UKQ" as a partial but not complete license plate number. Based on the witnesses coming forward, a search warrant was obtained for Bernard Phillip Hatch, who lived in a trailer with his sister and brother-in-law on Soule Road, Holland Patent, New York.

PREVIOUS CONVICTION AND SUSPECTED OF OTHER MURDERS

The search warrant was based on Hatch having been a paroled offender, having served six years in state prison for kidnapping, abduction and weapon charges. Bernard Phillip Hatch had served as a marine before returning to the Mohawk Valley in the early '60s. He was known to local police authorities at the time the search warrant was issued for the murder of Mary Rose Turner. He had been arrested in 1964 for the abduction of a teenage girl. Joseph Duffy, twenty, of Rome and Madeline Lazio, seventeen, of Frankfort were in a car parked in the lover's lane wooded area off Frankfort Gorge Road when Hatch came upon them with a .45-caliber pistol drawn. Hatch made them exit the vehicle, tied Duffy to a tree, fired a shot over his head with the pistol and then forced the girl to accompany him by gunpoint. Hatch was arrested, tried and sentenced by Judge Edmund A. McCarthy to a total of forty years, twenty-five years on the kidnapping charge, ten years on the abduction and five years on the weapons charge, with a minimum of sixteen and a half years to be served before he would be eligible for parole. The judge stated that Hatch had strayed from the motto of the Marine Corps, "Semper Fidelis," which means "Always Faithful."

Phillip Bernard Hatch was paroled much sooner than that, though. In addition to the previous arrest, Hatch had been suspected by police and questioned in the murder of Joanne Pechone, eighteen, of Utica, New York, who had been stabbed to death in January 1972. Hatch was never officially charged with this crime. The Mary Rose Turner Latteiman Road grave site soon had a companion: eight and a half months after troopers dug up Turner, they discovered four hundred feet away the grave site of Linda Cady, twenty-two, and her three-year-old son. The coroner ruled Cady's death as a homicide. Her legs had been tied together at the ankles. Troopers were also looking in the area for Lorraine Zinicola, twenty-five, and her three sons (ages two, four and seven), all of whom had gone missing in July 1971. Although law enforcement officials had their suspicions, Hatch was never charged with any of these deaths and disappearances.

THE SEARCH WARRANT AND ARREST

Troopers descended on the trailer where Bernard Phillip Hatch lived with his sister, Victoria Palcini, twenty-nine, and her husband, John Pulcini. Troopers confiscated newspaper articles on the crime that had been cut out and placed in a dresser drawer, as well as a pair of size-ten tan work boots that had human hairs on them, a pair of pants that had what appeared to be a bloodstain on them, a knife and sheath with human hairs in the sheath and rope in a shed. The police also impounded the 1966 green Plymouth that Hatch drove. Bernard Phillip Hatch was arrested and taken to the Oneida County Jail to await official murder charges and trial.

THE TRIAL AND THE PROSECUTION

Oneida County Court judge John J. Walsh was on the bench, while Edward A. Wolff Jr. was assigned to prosecute Hatch. Stephen Pawlinga was retained to be the defense attorney for Hatch, and his courtroom chess match with Wolff would become legal legend. The jury selection of ten men and two women was the quick and easy part as the trial got underway on November 6, 1974. The trial featured numerous witnesses, including New York state trooper Michael J. Jasek, from the identification bureau for Troop D, Oneida, who testified that he had

Bernard Phillip Hatch. *Oneida County Historical Society.*

inspected Bernard Phillip Hatch's 1966 green Plymouth that had been seized and taken to the Oneida barracks garage. Trooper Jasek found three knives in the trunk and two cans of lighter fluid in the glove box. He had dusted for fingerprints yet had found the car wiped completely clean.

The most important witness was the farmer, James Weaver, of Steuben, who testified that he was the person who had seen the white object being dragged behind Hatch's green car on Potato Hill Road and had been the person who called authorities when he saw blood and drag marks. He testified that he was about one thousand feet away from Potato Hill Road located by a set of power lines, yet when police officially measured the distance, it was four hundred feet.

Apparently, Hatch had confessed his crime while he sat in Oneida County Jail, for a witness for the prosecution, Joseph Nowak, came forth with information and testified on the stand. Nowak claimed that Hatch had admitted to him while they were cellmates at the Oneida County Jail that he had dragged Mary Rose Turner behind his car over several Steuben roads. Nowak even claimed that Hatch had recommended that he hire Pawlinga as his defense attorney, but the man had said that he couldn't afford the top-notch defender. According to Nowak, Hatch had said that Pawlinga was so accomplished a defense attorney that he had committed murder and would get away with it.

Pawlinga was good at attacking the credibility of Nowak and pointed out to the jury that the thirty-four-year-old had dropped out of Utica Free Academy as a sophomore, had a lengthy criminal past having served in Oneida County, Montgomery County and Herkimer County in the past year and previously had been incarcerated in Indiana on a bad check charge. On the stand, Nowak also testified and admitted to passing bad checks in several states and that he was in the army but was discharged for refusing to follow orders. He then rejoined the army using the name of a friend who had died and was AWOL at the time of the Hatch trial.

Several witnesses came forward to testify that they saw Hatch driving his green car the morning of the murder. Yvonne Farney of Soule Road testified that she had been walking a yearling horse on Soule Road the morning of the murder and had stopped at a neighbor's house when she saw Hatch's 1966 green Plymouth being spray-cleaned. She then witnessed Hatch placing items from the car in a can. Farney then testified that, later that night, there was a fire on the foundation of a burned-out home on Soule Road. A couple days later, she observed Hatch retrieving the items in the fire and placing them in the trunk of his car.

It was revealed that there was another green car on Latteiman Road on the day of the murder—perhaps this was the person everyone saw. William Kent testified, however, that he was fishing that day and had been on the road, yet his station wagon was a robin's egg blue and not green. Jerry Boak testified that on April 28, he changed the tires on Hatch's green Plymouth at a Holland Patent service station. He removed large oval tires and replaced them with regular tires. Witnesses had testified to seeing Hatch's car with the distinctive oversized oval tires, including Stephen C. Earl of Boonville, who testified to seeing a green, clean and shiny car at 11:50 a.m. on Latteiman Road, moving at a high rate of speed. State police investigator Leo Bartowiak identified photos of Bernard Phillip Hatch's car in 1972. Richard Rintona, who employed Hatch as a carpenter's assistant, testified that Hatch did not report to work on the day Mary Rose Turner was murdered and had called in to say that he needed the day off since his mother was sick so he couldn't work.

Part of Hatch's defense was that he was with his mother in Deansboro at the time of the murder, had gone with her to pick out a car and had even visited a television repair shop in Waterville, thus giving him an alibi for the entire morning. Mrs. Anne Alsheimer of Waterville, a television store owner, testified that Mrs. Hatch's television had never been brought in to be repaired on the morning of April 26, 1973, because she never opened her store before noon. Hatch's brother-in-law and sister had claimed that they were there the morning of the murder. Ralph Marcucio, chemist, testified that there was a blood spot found on Hatch's tan whipcord pants, which he had been wearing when the troopers searched the trailer. He identified the spot as human blood, but it was too small to verify that it was Mary Rose Turner's blood. Pawlinga was able to get the chemist to admit that he was not 100 percent certain that the hairs found on the knife sheath and the hair on Hatch's boots, as well as the hair on the rope found near the grave site, were Turner's. The chemist could only testify that they were similar in type to Mary Rose Turner.

THE DEFENSE

Bernard Phillip Hatch's mother, Florence Hatch, seventy, took the stand in her son's defense and testified that "Bobby" went to bed at 9:15 a.m. the day of the murder and didn't get up until 11:00 a.m. Her son had come to stay with her in Deansboro for a short time instead of living at the trailer with his sister and brother-in-law. Florence then testified that her daughter came over and that the three of them went to Dodge City in Yorkville, New York, to look at cars. Hatch's mother also stated that her son was born in Goshen and that the family moved to Steuben in 1946 when she purchased three hundred acres of farmland on Bowen Hill on the east side of Potato Hill Road near the intersection of Latteiman Road. Police investigators pointed out that Hatch knew the area well since he had lived there.

Hatch's sister, Victoria Palcini, then testified that newspaper clippings of the murder that police had found in a dresser drawer in the trailer had been clipped by her and belonged to her. She also stated that police had been harassing her brother since they tagged him as a suspect in the murder of Joanne Pecheone of Utica, New York, who had been stabbed to death.

Hatch's daughter, Cassie, was called to the stand, and the teenager testified that she had been questioned by police the day they came to the trailer with a search warrant. Hatch's brother-in-law, John Pulcini, testified that the tan boots that had human hairs on them—which the troopers had confiscated in the search warrant—were his. Pulcini testified that Hatch had borrowed the boots in the past. Pulcini then testified that Hatch was home all morning, for he saw Hatch's feet sticking out as he slept, and that Hatch's green Plymouth never left the driveway. John Pulicini refused to take a polygraph test when asked by police investigators and also refused to sign a written statement.

Rosemary Snyder and her mother, Mrs. Cora Snyder, testified that they had seen Hatch driving on Soule Road, Holland Patent, the morning of the murder, so he couldn't have been over on Potato Hill Road, Steuben. Bernard Phillip Hatch claimed that he had seen the ladies that morning around the time of the dragging. Rosemary Snyder testified that she was in love with Hatch.

Bernard Phillip Hatch took the stand in his own defense and testified that he had heard about the murder on Saturday, April 28, 1973, two days after the crime, through a fellow employee where he worked at the Boehling Shell Gas Station on Court Street, Utica, New York. Hatch stated that because of the murder and because the cops had gone to his trailer, he went to stay with his mother. "With everything considered, I felt the best place for me was not at the garage," said Hatch from the stand. It was revealed that Mary Rose Turner had lived nearby the gas station where Hatch had worked. Hatch testified that he was never questioned by police in the murder of Joanne Pechone, but cops buying gas at the station told him that he was being investigated for the murder. Hatch admitted that the knife and sheath that had the hairs similar to Mary Rose Turner were his. In his closing statement, Pawlinga asked the jury not to buy into the media hype and explained that there was no direct evidence that Hatch had committed the crime—in fact, the entire bulk of evidence was circumstantial. "If you have already made up your minds on guilty because of pre-trial publicity, then you are no better than whoever committed this crime," said Pawlinga. The defense attorney also attacked the testimony of Joseph Nowak, who had said that Hatch admitted to the crime in the Oneida County Jail.

THE VERDICT

The jury was handed the case and asked by Judge Walsh to come back with either innocent or guilty. He stated to the jury, "Sympathy, prejudice, and bias are human emotions but they have no place in the courtroom or the jury room." Judge Walsh paused and then completed his statement to the jury: "A defendant is upon the evidence and the evidence alone, either guilty or innocent." After many months of witnesses and mounds of testimony and evidence to peruse, the members of the jury went into deliberations. They had been asked ahead of time by the judge to bring nightclothes and toiletries in case they couldn't come to a verdict and had to spend the night sequestered in a local hotel.

The jury deliberated for four hours that first day before quitting for the night. They had dinner together that night at a local hotel. The deliberations resumed the next day at 9:30 a.m., with the jury at noontime requesting part of the stenographer's typed testimony, along with the photos of Mary Rose Turner's limbless, toothless, faceless corpse that had been determined to have been dragged nine miles down Potato Hill Road. An hour before the verdict was read, Hatch's mother held up a picture in the courtroom of a young, clean-shaven soldier. "This is the real Bernard Hatch," she said. "A good man not the bum and the animal they've made him out to be. What that little girl [Cassandra] has been through in unbelievable. The pointing, the stares, losing her friends. She has no trust left. And she's much too old for 16. Too old."

The jury came back with a verdict. Jury foreman Terence Kehoe stood and announced to a silent and packed courtroom: "Guilty." The verdict was read at 2:50 p.m. on Friday, March 7, 1975. Bernard Phillip Hatch faced at a minimum fifteen to twenty-five years at Attica State Prison or a maximum of life. Hatch was reported to be calm when the verdict was read. Judge Walsh thanked the jury, and Hatch's mother broke out in tears, along with his daughter Cassandra. Hatch's sister leaned her head onto her mother's shoulder, her eyes wet with tears. "I can't stand it. I can't stand it," said Cassandra to her grandmother as she consoled her granddaughter with unrecognizable whispers. Hatch was taken away to the Oneida County Jail, while Pawlinga escorted Hatch's family to the courtroom elevator.

POST CONVICTION

The trial of Bernard Phillip Hatch was the lengthiest and most expensive in the history of Oneida County at sixty-seven days of testimony, a span from November 1974 until March 1975, and it came in at a cost of about $1 million. There was close to eight thousand pages of court transcripts. The jury was composed of the foreman, Terence Kehoe; Louise Madden, Sherill; Arthur Woodruff, Rome; Orlando E. Cicotti, Rome; James Hellig, Rome; Willis H. Carr, New Hartford; Kenneth G. Holliday, Oriskany; Jack J. Delaney, North Bay; Mary Servatius; Wesley Vanderhorst, Clinton; Henry C. Spelliey, Camden; and David G. Farnsworth, Camden. Bernard Phillip Hatch was sent to Oneida County Jail to await his sentencing, and it was here where he cut his left wrist with a razor that he had taken by slipping his arm between the bars and into an adjacent bathroom. He didn't cut any of his main veins, and the guards found him immediately.

Sheriff Hasenauer said that "Bernie doesn't talk much. It's impossible to tell what's going on in the mind of a man who is awaiting sentencing." Bernard Phillip Hatch was sentenced to twenty-five years to life and was sent to the Auburn Correctional Facility. Thirty-seven years later, in the summer of 2010, Hatch was denied parole. The members of the parole board released a statement explaining why they denied Hatch his freedom. They stated that despite Hatch's claim that he was innocent, his good behavior in prison and much correspondence from supporters, it wasn't enough to overcome the malicious violence he had shown Mary Rose Turner. "Your release would be incompatible with the welfare of society and would so deprecate the serious nature of the crime as to undermine respect for the law," noted the parole board in the released statement.

BERNARD PHILLIP HATCH PRISON
INTERVIEW REQUEST

The author wrote to Bernard Phillip Hatch in the summer of 2011 requesting an interview at the Auburn correctional facility. The goal was to have the man explain his self-proclaimed innocence. As of the writing of this book, there had been no answer from Bernard Phillip Hatch.

The Mohawk Valley County Dossier

These are the counties that make up the Mohawk Valley of Central New York.

FULTON COUNTY

Fulton County, which was created on April 18, 1838, was named after Robert Fulton, who was the first commercially successful person to employ a steamboat. Mr. Fulton's cousin was married to Johnstown attorney Daniel Cady, who was instrumental in the county's formation. The Old Tryon County Courthouse, which later became the Montgomery County Courthouse and then finally the Fulton County Courthouse, is the oldest operating courthouse in New York State. The hardworking citizens of Fulton County are the direct descendants of the glove manufacturing employees who settled in Gloversville and Johnstown to improve their lives with steady, well-paying employment. In this county, criminality and ballyhoo are frowned upon by an upstanding, blue-collar populace.

HERKIMER COUNTY

Herkimer County was named after the Revolutionary War general Nicholas Herkimer, who died in 1777 from wounds he had received in the Battle of Oriskany. The county is a skinny but lengthy one that touches the Adirondack

Mountain blue line to the north and has the Mohawk River cutting through the south. Herkimer is also known around the world for its high-quality doubly terminated quartz crystals, referred to as Herkimer Diamonds.

MONTGOMERY COUNTY

Montgomery County was originally named Tryon County in 1772 and was broken up into smaller counties, with the name being changed to Montgomery in 1784 to honor the Revolutionary War general Richard Montgomery, who died bravely in battle trying to capture the city of Quebec. The county's main seat is Fonda, due to the Erie Canal being dug right through the center. The area was originally settled by the Dutch, who worked their farms hard and were especially exceptional at producing grains. These early settlers sowed the seeds of democracy. This was an area of integrity for standard-bearing citizens who had no time for those who ran afoul of the law.

ONEIDA COUNTY

Oneida County sits in the midst of the Mohawk Valley and has the two largest cities in Utica and Rome. It was formed in 1798 when it split from Herkimer County. It has Oneida Lake bordering on one end and the Adirondack Mountain blue line on the other, with the Barge Canal running straight through. The county is known for its diverse population due to immigrants and refugees coming in from all over the globe. The Revolutionary War made its mark with the Battle of Oriskany, and the village of Old Fort Schuyler became Utica in the early nineteenth century when Erastus Clark wrote the name on a piece of paper and placed it in a hat at Bagg's Tavern. This set the flavorful tone for Oneida County that continues to this day.

SCHENECTADY COUNTY

Schenectady County is actually part of the Albany-Troy metropolitan statistical area, yet it is considered a part of the Mohawk Valley. The name is from a Mohawk Indian word that means "on the other side of the pine lands." It was formed as a county in 1809 and is the first county you hit as you travel north from Albany.

SCHOHARIE COUNTY

Schoharie County was named after a Mohawk word that means "floating driftwood." The county was founded in 1795, and the seat is the town of Schoharie. Here is the location of the Old Stone Fort, which was once a church that was converted and used to defend against the British in the Revolutionary War.

Appendix B

Map of the Mohawk Valley

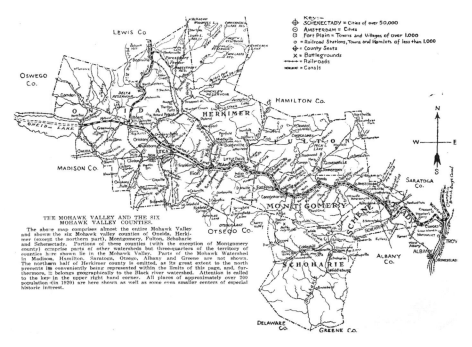

A 1920 map of the Mohawk Valley, from *History of the Mohawk Valley*, volume I, by Nelson Greene. *Oneida County Historical Society.*

Bibliography

Amsterdam (NY) Evening Recorder & Daily Democrat. "Italian Witnesses Break Jail at Fonda." June 3, 1909.

———. "Judge M'Lachlan Found Murdered." July 24 1907.

———. "Jury Acquits Frank Denatto." June 19, 1909.

———. "Sheriff Jackson Makes Denial of Removal Charges." May 15, 1936.

Bagg, M.M., MD. *Memorial History of Utica, New York.* Syracuse, NY: D. Mason & Company Publishers, 1892.

Bean, Phillip A. *The Urban Colonists Italian American Identity & Politics in Utica, New York.* Syracuse, NY: Syracuse University Press, 2010.

Bean, Phillip, and Gene Nassar. *Rufie: A Political Scrapbook.* Utica, NY: Ethnic Heritage Studies Center, Utica College, 2009.

Binghamton (NY) Press. "Dogs Are Put on Fugitive's Trail." January 8, 1921.

Case, Richard G. "The Hanging of a Murderess." *Legacy, Annals of Herkimer County,* no. 1 (1987): 3–9.

Ellis, David Maldwyn. *The Upper Mohawk Country*. Woodland Hills, CA: Windsor Publications, 1982.

Foote, Allan D. *Liberty March: The Battle of Oriskany.* Utica, NY: North Country Books, 1998.

Gloversville and Johnstown (NY) Morning Herald. "Bert Peck, on Trial for Abortion, Found Guilty by Jury in County Court." February 5, 1931.

———. "Court Reopens for Peck Trial." February 7, 1931.

———. "Evidence at Variance with Original Affidavit Given in Peck's Abortion Action." February 4, 1931.

———. "Governor Lehman Orders Investigation of Charges Against Sheriff Jackson." July 23, 1936.

———. "Indictments Found by Jury for Alleged Poison Liquor Death of Mrs. Lena Snyder." April 4, 1935.

———. "Investigator Resigns Post." April 1, 1936.

———. "Lehman Orders Jackson to Reply to Charges Preferred by Three Former Officials." April 22, 1936.

———. "Mrs. Derrico Pleads Guilty to Manslaughter in Second Degree, First Day of Court." May 21, 1935.

———. "Police Chief George Smith Challenges Anyone to Prove He Has Taken a Cent of Graft." February 13, 1935.

———. "Sheriff Jackson Files Refutation of Charges with Governor Lehman." May 16, 1936.

Greene, Nelson. *History of the Mohawk Valley.* Volume I. Chicago: St. Clark Publishing Company, 1925.

Kingston (NY) Daily Freeman. "Man, Wife Are Arrested for Brothel Charges." March 7, 1958.

Lowville (NY) Journal and Republican. "Jurymen Failed to Do Duty." June 11, 1914.

New York Times. "Bares Chum's Plot to Kill Teacher." March 30, 1914.

———. "Differ About Gianini. Alienists Disagree as to His Understanding His Crime." May 20, 1914.

———. "Gianini Confesses; Insanity His Plea." March 31, 1914.

———. "Teacher Killed Had Befriended Him, Miss Beecher Was Trying to Have Gianini Admitted to George Junior Republic." April 1, 1914.

Oswego (NY) Daily Times. "Boy Wreckers Trial." April 20, 1896.

———. "In Hildreth's Behalf." May 6, 1896.

Otsego Farmer. "Chicken Roost Gang Now in Schoharie Jail, Wanted Locally." July 17, 1936.

The People History. "What Happened in 1936." http://www.thepeoplehistory.com/1936.html.

Pistone, Joseph D. *The Way of the Wiseguy.* Philadelphia, PA: Running Press, 2004.

Schenectady (NY) Gazette. "Local Woman Slays Son With Axe; Feared for His Commitment to Institution." August 13, 1947.

———. "Mrs. Grabo Sent to Matteawan by Judge." August 14, 1947.

———. "Reali Murder Case Jury Expected to Begin Deliberations Today." December 19, 1944.

———. "Reali's Widow Takes Stand as Murder Trial Testimony Starts." December 8, 1944.

———. "Rossi and Stendor Get 35 Years to Life Terms." December 21, 1944.

———. "Youths Confess Brutal Slaying of Edward Reali." August 14, 1944.

Syracuse (NY) Daily Journal. "Kept His Hideous Sorrows to Self. Gianini's Wife and Daughter Never Knew Life History of Jean's Mother." May 16, 1914.

Syracuse (NY) Post Standard. "Boy, 17, Under Arrest Charged with Murder of His Former Teacher." March 30, 1914.

———. "Can't Give Me More than Ten Years Boy States to Constable." May 13, 1914.

———. "Jury Out Many Hours with Case of Gianini." May 28, 1914.

Syracuse Daily Courier. "Vindicated! Mrs. Roxalana Druse Executed." March 1, 1887.

Syracuse Journal. "She 'Snitched' So I Killed Her, Says Boy Slayer." May 19, 1914.

Thomas, Alexander R. *In Gotham's Shadow: Globalization and Community Change in Central New York.* Albany: State University of New York Press, 2003.

Utica (NY) Daily Press. "Basile, Associate of Malkoons, Taken for a Ride." April 15, 1931.

———. "Boy Is Held for Murder." March 30, 1914.

———. "The Boy Train Wreckers." 1896.

———. "Brothel Operators to Be Sentenced Friday in Rome." March 24, 1959.

———. "Footwear Testimony Heard in Hatch Case." February 26, 1975.

———. "Found Rope on Hitch, Trooper Testifies." January 24, 1975.

———. "Gianini Is Not Guilty." May, 29, 1914.

Bibliography

————. "Hamlin Asks Valachi Crime Data." October 12, 1963.

————. "Hatch a Suspect Before Mrs. Turner's Body Was Found." January 14, 1975.

————. "Hatch Case May Go to Jury Today." March 5, 1975.

————. "Hatch Cuts His Wrist; Wound Called Small." April 3, 1975.

————. "Hatch Given 25 Yrs. to Life." August 4, 1964.

————. "Hatch Jury Quits for Night." March 7, 1975.

————. "Hatch Jury Sequestered on Eve of Deliberations." March 6, 1975.

————. "High Court Clears Falcones." December 10, 1940.

————. "Joseph Falcone Gives Up; Sought Since '58." August 18, 1962.

————. "Man Testifies to Seeing Green Car." January 15, 1975.

————. "Miami Hearing Set for Henry Cittadino, Wife." March 8, 1958.

————. "Mother, Sister Take Stand for Accused Man." February 27, 1975.

————. "60th Day Today in Hatch's Trial." February 19, 1975.

————. "State Revokes Licenses Held By Falcone." March 29, 1958.

————. "Testimony Expected to End Monday in Hatch Case." March 1, 1975.

————. "Turner Murder Case Cost Nearly $1 Million." March 9, 1975.

————. "Virgil Jackson's Trial." April 11, 1888.

————. "Witness Tells of Conversation with Hatch." February 4, 1975.

Utica (NY) Observer Dispatch. "Apalachin Today: Who Remembers?" November 28, 1982.

———. "Cittadino, Conte Get Jail Terms." April 19, 1944.

———. "The Court House Is My Beat." December 6, 1983.

———. "Elefante Didn't Pick Slate, Pawlinga Says." July 27, 1961.

———. "Elefante Remains a Dominant Force." 1981.

———. "Hanna, Elefante Talk Set." April 6, 1974.

———. "New Brothel Case Indictments Possible." January 23, 1958.

———. "Power-Shy Elefante: The Mayor Is the Boss." September 29, 1974.

———. "Three Held in Poison Case Enter Pleas of Not Guilty." February 8. 1935.

Utica (NY) Saturday Globe. "Borst Badly Wanted, Criminal Record Long." January 21, 1921.

———. "Foul Play Charged." January 7, 1910.

———. "No Jury Yet." 1896.

———. "They Escape the Chair." May 9 1896.

———. "Those Young Demons at Rome!" November 23, 1895.

Utica (NY) Weekly Herald & Gazette and Courier. "Expiation! A Woman Hanged in Herkimer." March 1, 1887.

———. "Premeditated." April 17, 1888.

———. "Scandal Destroys Body and Soul." April 7, 1916.

———. "Whiskey Scandal Brings Federal Agents to Utica." April 19, 1920.

Waterville Times. "To Mary Runkle Goes a Dubious Honor." January 7, 1998

Wikipedia. "Fulton County, New York." http://en.wikipedia.org/wiki/Fulton_County_New_York.

———. "Gloversville, New York." http://en.wikipedia.org/wiki/Gloversville_New_York.

———. "Herkimer County, New York." http://en.wikipedia.org/wiki/Fulton_County_New_York.

———. "Montgomery County, New York." http://en.wikipedia.org/wiki/Montgomery_County_New_York.

———. "Oneida County, New York." http://en.wikipedia.org/wiki/Oneida_County_New_York.

———. "Schenectady County, New York." http://en.wikipedia.org/wiki/Schenectady_County_New_York.

———. "Schoharie County, New York." http://en.wikipedia.org/wiki/Schoharie_County_New_York.

Williams, Robert Hunter. "Dirt Storm in Utica." Chap. 3 in *Vice Squad*. New York: Crowell Press, 1973.

About the Author

Dennis Webster was born, lives, works and plays in the Mohawk Valley of Central New York. He received his bachelor of science degree from Utica College and his master of business administration (MBA) degree from the State University of New York Institute of Technology at Utica/Rome. He's the author of *Haunted Mohawk Valley*; compiler, editor and story contributor to the Tommy Award Honorable Mention anthology *Adirondack Mysteries*, along with *Adirondack Mysteries 2*; and is the author of the fiction novel *Daisy Daring and the Quest for the Loomis Gang Gold*. He can be reached at denniswbstr@gmail.com.

Visit us at
www.historypress.net